M000224280

2nd CHANCE at LIFE

Kenneth Hough

ISBN 978-1-0980-9890-2 (paperback)
ISBN 978-1-0980-9891-9 (digital)

Christian Faith Publishing, Inc.
832 Park Avenue
Meadville, PA 16335
www.christianfaithpublishing.com

Printed in the United States of America

I wrote this book so people can have a better understanding of what some cardiac arrest victims go through and try to help them and their loved ones through a journey that wrecks them mentally and physically. At the time that my cardiac arrest occurred, I got an epidural injection in my neck for a work-related accident that happened a year prior. Being discharged from the hospital a day later didn't seem like the proper protocol to me for someone who has just flat-lined and sustained severe bruising from CPR being administered. No in-depth testing was done to make sure that I wasn't suffering from any neurological or physical damages, not even any therapy or discharge to an outpatient center.

It was definitely a slow process getting the authorizations needed for all the medical treatments, doctors, MRIs, and medications in a timely manner. The clock is ticking, and not receiving the proper medical treatment quickly can be devastating and can cause other problems. Take a walk with me as I relive my horror to tell you my story. This is also my testimony.

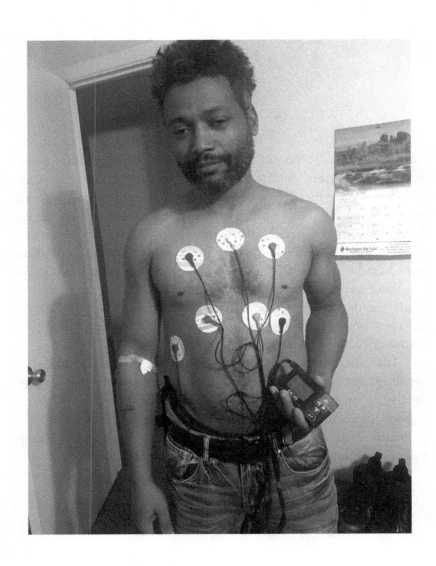

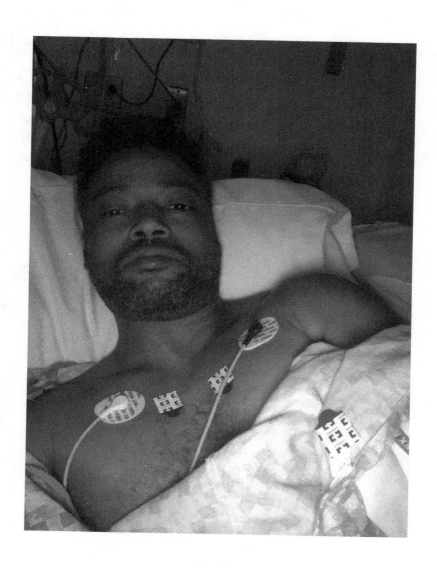

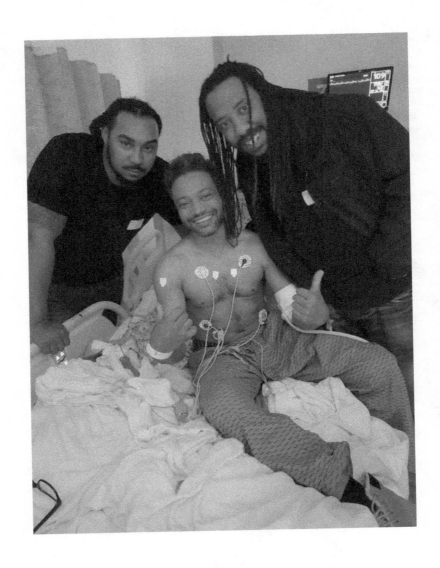

The date was February 15, 2019, and the alarm went off at 5:00 a.m., and I was awakened to start what I considered usually a normal day and did my usual routine in the mornings. I used the bathroom, washed my hands, brushed my teeth, washed my face, and greased and brushed my hair while in the process of getting dressed. I called my sister to let her know that I was up and would be on my way to pick her up by 5:45 a.m. And I walked over to my wife's side of the bed and gave her a kiss on her cheek and told her I loved her and for her to have a good day at work, like I usually do every morning while leaving to go to work due to the fact that I have to be up early and out the door before she got up.

I grabbed my wallet and keys, put on my jacket, and as I was headed toward the door, I started to have a funny feeling about going to get this epidural procedure. Usually my wife takes me, but for some odd reason, she refused to take me that day. So that's why I had my sister take me. I didn't know what it was, but I was feeling like I shouldn't get this epidural shot. I brushed the feeling off as I locked my door and headed toward my truck. I started up the Mountaineer, turned the radio to 95.5 FM as I warmed the truck up.

I usually don't eat breakfast since I get up early, but today I was feeling hungry and was craving everything. So I drove across the street to 7-Eleven to get something to eat. I didn't know what I wanted, so I grabbed a Kit Kat knowing that the doctor said specifically to not eat or drink anything after 12:00 a.m., the night before the procedure. I would just keep the Kit Kat in the truck and eat it after my procedure. As I left the 7-Eleven and got back into the Mountaineer, I drove to my sister's house, which is literally ten minutes from where I stay. As I was coming up her street, I grabbed my phone and called my sister to let her know I was outside.

My sister came out and got in the truck, and we headed on out toward Interstate 95 en route toward the outpatient center, the same one I had been going to for some time now to alleviate the pains from my work-related injury. It's been a whole year since I had the injury, and the pain was still unbearable. Doctors tried almost everything but surgery to help me alleviate the pains, but nothing they suggested or did was helping me.

Physical therapy was the first thing they tried, and it didn't help at all. If anything, physical therapy irritated my injury even more. I never knew you could actually twist and sprain your neck. Trying to pull a long box above my head out of a crate, it wouldn't budge as I tugged and tugged, and it finally came free as I lost my balance, trying to hold on and somehow jerked my neck resulting in two slipped disc and a spasm in my neck. Yeah, yeah, I know, right. Definitely not good. That left me with spinal cord compression on my C4 and C5 and also my C6 and C7 cervical vertebra. Medications ain't even helping with my pains.

My doctors also had me go see a physiatrists that gave me all types of medications to try. An orthopedic oncologist got me the nerve block, cervical rhizotomy, and the epidural shots. Nothing was working to manage my pains. The list of medications they had me taking were tizanidine, oxycodone, naproxen, hydrocodone, Lyrica, gabapentin, meloxicam, prednisone, cyclobenzaprine, and morphine pills up to this point. This would be my second epidural injection procedure but the fifth procedure with this anesthesiologists.

The pain was so unbearable, and there was nothing I could do about it. I had been just living with it and dealing with it without complaining. I was hoping these doctors would find a way to stop my pains or suppress it without getting any type of in-depth critical surgery done. Let me tell you all a little bit about the procedures they have done on my neck so far.

A nerve block is a procedure where they intentionally damage or cut the nerve to halt the pain messages coming from the nerves in a particular part of the body. A cervical rhizotomy is a procedure for treating nerve pains by sending pulses of heat energy generated by radio waves to the affected nerves to burn them out the way.

As my sister and I was riding on Interstate 95, I started thinking how different this morning was feeling without my wife taking me as we were getting closer to my destination. Usually she would take me, but for some odd reason, she had been against me getting this epidural injection done. She had been against this for weeks when I told her about it. She said, "Baby, it is not helping you with your pains. You need to stop going and letting them experiment on you.

You need to stop letting them stick needles in your neck and burning your nerves away." She started to become fearful and started praying for me.

I told my wife, "This will be the last time, baby. After this, I will tell my doctors that nothing is working and we need to try a different route for relieving my pains." My wife asked me to pray to God to take the pains away, and I became bitter. And I wasn't walking in God's faith at the time and told my wife, "Praying isn't going to take my pain away. The medications I'm taking isn't even helping, so what makes you think that praying is going to work?"

My wife is a God-fearing woman, but I wasn't a God-fearing man at the time. I was brought up in the church at a young age and baptized, but as I got older, I strayed away from religion and was living life of a sinner. I often went to church with my wife just to keep the peace but wasn't planning on giving my life to God.

So my sister started asking me a lot of questions about driving my truck because she never drove an SUV before. She didn't want to be uncomfortable driving me back home. I explained to her to picture it as driving an oversized car. It just sits up higher and is heavier, and she would be fine. We finally got to the outpatient center, and I signed in, ready for my 6:30 a.m. appointment. My sister and I were talking about ancient civilizations that school didn't teach you about. They finally called me back to get prepped and ready for my epidural injection with the anesthesiologist.

After laying on the gurney in my patient gown, the nurse came in and put the IV into my arm and asked me when the last time I ate, and I told her 9:00 p.m. last night. I was just steadily researching about the ancient Akkadians, Babylonians, and Sumerians and reading up on Enki and Enlil and some of the Anunnaki gods, and noticed I've been waiting for a while now and texted my wife to let her know I was in the back ready for them to do the procedure. The nurse came back and said the doctor was running late and as soon as he got in, I would be patient number two. So I said okay, no worries, and thought to myself, *Well, why was he running late though?* I asked myself, and my mind started wondering and thinking about everything. *Is this a sign? Was God trying to tell me something?*

I'm starting to have second thoughts about getting this epidural injection. Since I was already there, I might as well go on with the procedure. It was no use of backing out now. Finally, the doctor arrived, and it's finally my turn as the nurse came to get me and started pushing my gurney into the procedure room. And they told me to slide onto the procedure table face down. As I was adjusting my face into the cut out on the procedure table, the nurse put the oxygen line into my nostrils and started sterilizing my neck and upper back area with some type of solution.

I noticed some type of thick tape used to hold something down, and I asked what the duct tape was for. And one of the assistants said, "It's to hold your extremities down, so you wouldn't be moving irregularly while the doctor is giving you the epidural shot." The assistants grabbed the duct tape and applied the tape from one shoulder across my body to my opposite leg, and at that moment, one of the nurses said, "I put the solution in the IV," and at that moment, I blacked out.

I started hearing voices, but I was having a hard time understanding what I was hearing. Everything sounded muffled surrounded in pitch-blackness. As I tried to open my eyes, it felt as if an unseen force was holding my eyes shut. Almost like a veil was placed over my eyes. It felt like hot hands while I was laying on my back. It felt as if it was fifteen unseen people holding me down with both sets of hands. It felt like hands were all over my body—little hands, big hands, all type of hands, as if they were trying to pull me down.

As I tried to get up, the unseen force would not let me. The more I fought to get up, the more the unseen force got stronger. I fought to free my legs. But the unseen force stopped me. I fought to free my arms and hands, but the unseen force stopped me, I couldn't get loose. I started to tire and panic. At that moment, I just knew something was not right. As I was about to give up, I heard a faint voice telling me to not give up. And at this point, I knew giving up wasn't an option. I became afraid, so I fought more and more with this unseen force. And it felt like I got stronger and stronger, and the unseen force couldn't keep his grip on me. Finally, I was free.

As I opened my eyes from the darkness, the room was bright. As I tried adjusting my eyes, I noticed I was being rushed down a corridor on a gurney. I was trying my best to figure out where I was because this place didn't look familiar to me. As my vision started coming in, I noticed I was being pushed through the emergency room of a hospital. It was paramedics all around the gurney, and one kept talking to me. I was so much in a daze. My thoughts were drowning in a pool of confusion. The left cavity of my chest felt as if I drank a whole fifth of Bacardi Rum 151.

My chest was on fire from some type of pain that I had no idea how it got there. The paramedic finally caught my attention. He started asking me could I hear him. And I could hear him, and I tried to reply, but I couldn't talk. Every word I tried to say came out my mouth sounding like mumble jumble. And the more I tried talking, the more mumble jumble started coming out. I started to get frustrated.

The paramedics finally got me in a room at the end of the corridor to the right, and I was left in there holding my chest and moaning. The pain was so unbearable. I started crying and praying for God to stop the pain and take it away from me. I was left alone for some time when I noticed the curtain open up, and my sister walked in. I said to her in a painful voice, "What happened? Why am I here? Why is my chest in so much pain?"

My sister said, "You died! They had to revive you!"

And I responded with, "What you mean I died?" And at that moment, the curtain opened up again, and a male doctor walked into the room and started talking to my sister while I'm turning from side to side, holding the left side of my chest with my left hand and moaning. After talking with my sister briefly, the doctor then told me that I went into cardiac arrest and that's why I was there. I asked him why my chest was on fire and in pain, and he said probably due to the CPR performed on me to save my life and said he could give me some fentanyl to help with the pain, so he injected some into my IV and said they need to run some tests on me and told my sister that I would be back shortly.

11

A nurse came into the room and pushed my gurney out into the corridor and down another hall through some double doors, and at that time I asked, "Where are you taking me?"

She responded, "I'm taking you to get a CT scan of your head." She pushed my gurney down another hall and told the tech, "Here's Mr. Hough," and walked off. The technician took me into the room and helped me off the gurney onto the machine to get my head scanned all while starting small conversation with me about why I was there for the scan. Not really in the mood to be talking, but I told the technician that I had a cardiac arrest while getting an epidural injection in my neck.

The technician said, "Oh my goodness, you look too young to be experiencing this! I will pray for you." The technician scanned my head and helped me back into my gurney and paged for the nurse to come and get me. After a few minutes, the nurse came and got me to take me back to my room. My sister walked back in with a worried look upon her face and kept asking me if I was alright, and she contacted my wife and she should be here shortly.

I told my sister, "Hell no, I'm not alright! I'm in pain!" By this time, my wife had arrived and walked into the room. While clutching my chest, I looked up at my wife, and her face showed a sign of pure terror as if she was looking at a ghost. My sister embraced my wife, calmed her down, and started to explain to her all that has transpired.

At that moment, the doctor came back into the room and said, "The CT scan is showing that you have an aneurysm of the brain and brain hemorrhage, and we don't have the equipment to further help you."

In anger, I started blurting out curse words and swearing while saying, "I got what? If I have anything, it's your fault." The doctor asked me if I wanted some more fentanyl for my pain, and I said, "Hell yeah." He called the nurse in, and she injected me with more fentanyl.

The doctor came back into the room and told everyone that he was transferring me to another hospital located in Washington, DC, that had the equipment I needed for my diagnosis to help me, and the nurse was contacting a transport now and they would be driving me instead of flying me in a helicopter. It seemed like the medicine was not helping with my chest pains as they seem to get more intense. The transport finally arrived, and three EMTs walked into the room and prepped me to take me to another facility in the city for my complications. They rolled me out to the ambulance in the gurney and got me inside and strapped me down for the thirty-minute ride to the city.

Just five minutes into the ride, and my head started to feel like someone was beating on it like a drum, and the chest pains became more intense as I rolled my head back in forth in anguish. The tech asked if I wanted some more fentanyl and that it was enough for one shot left that the doctor gave him. And you already know what my answer was. I said once again, "Hell yeah."

Before I get into the story any deeper, I will refer to the hospitals by numbers instead of names. So finally, we arrived to hospital number two, and the techs got me down out the ambulance and pushed me through the doors into the emergency room. And the doctors showed them what room to put me in. Talking about being crowded, sheesh! They had patients in gurneys all over the place, looking like a scene to a movie. The only problem is that I was the one living this horror.

My sister and wife followed the ambulance along the journey and found their way into the room I was being kept in. I looked at their faces, and I could see the tears rolling down my wife's cheeks as she was grateful that I didn't check out of here for good. And my sister just had a look of shock that I will never forget as long as I live. I got to say through all of this, my sister kept her cool while calling all our immediate family members. While waiting on the doctor, I gave my wife my phone and told her that I need her to make a few calls for me, call my elevator union, and let them know what has happened to me, my supervisor, my company risk management case nurse, and my kids.

By this time, while my sister and wife were making their calls, the doctor came in the room to talk to us to get a better understanding to what's going on and how it happened. The funny thing is that

I don't even know what really happened. All of this just doesn't seem real to me. The reality of this injury hasn't hit me yet. All I know is that I was getting an epidural injection at an outpatient center, and I woke up in pain in hospital number one in Maryland.

My sister got off the phone and explained to the doctor everything that had transpired to allow me to rest since my voice was still weak. The doctor let us know that he would do all the proper medical scans I needed to check my heart, my brain, and my neck and would get the ball rolling and a nurse would be in soon to come and get me. And the doctor stepped out. While waiting, I was talking to my wife and listened to her tell me how that call from my sister almost turned her life upside down. While she was at work and the call from my sister after learning what happened, she immediately told her supervisor, jumped in her car, and was driving like she was on a NASCAR track trying to qualify for a big race. My work phone rang, and my wife answered.

"Hello," and she said, "Baby, it's your attorney calling. Your union hall phoned him and told him what was going on."

And I said, "Attorney?"

And my wife said, "Yeah, your workers comp attorney."

And I said, "Oh, I totally forgot about him. I talked to him about a year ago about my work-related injury."

Suddenly, this lady came into my room and said my name, and I responded with a yes. And she said, "Oh, I thought I was coming to get and do a death report. I didn't know that you survived your cardiac arrest. Usually when I'm called to do a follow-up on cardiac arrests victims, they don't survive the ordeal." She sounded disappointed.

This lady was a worker's compensation nurse that's apparently supposed to be working my case. After asking all the necessary questions she needed answers to, she said that she will keep in touch and left. My wife got upset and said, "Who is this woman?"

And I said, "She said she is my worker's comp nurse. I've never met her before." Thirty minutes later, a nurse came in the room to take me to get a CT scan of my brain to check for that aneurism that I was supposed to have. So I told my wife that I will be back, so the nurse wheeled me out the room in the gurney as my wife finished up making her phone calls. While rolling through the corridors of hospital two, the nurse finally got me to the room to get my scan done. And after letting the tech know who I was, she said, "I will be back to get you when your scan is complete," and left.

The tech came out and verified all of my info, and after my acknowledgment of the info, the tech explained how the scan works and got me off the gurney and onto the machine for the scan, got me into position, and went back to his station to start the scan. I really couldn't remember how long the scan of my head and brain took because I was too busy praying to God and asking him to please don't let me have swelling on my brain and an aneurism. I didn't want to die!

While tears started to run away from my eyes, the tech came and told me that's it and that the doctor will explain the results and buzzed for the nurse to come and take me back to my room. While helping me back onto my gurney, the tech asked what's wrong and why I was here. And I responded with, "I had an epidural injection done and went into cardiac arrest."

And the tech said, "Oh my! You look too young to be going through that. I will pray for you." By now, the nurse came and took me back through the corridors and back to the ER, passing the horror scene of all the sick and injured on gurneys and chairs on both sides of this one particular corridor that I will never forget.

After returning to my room, my wife let me know that she had called everyone that I asked her to and my oldest sister and son have said that they would be arriving to visit me soon. At this time, the doctor came in to discuss my CT scan and said that my scan didn't show an aneurism. But it did show that I have pneumocephalus, which is just air in my cranial cavity, but it would dissipate gradually. And you know me, I wanted to know how air got in my brain and why my head was killing me. So I asked the doctor and he said, "It is possible to get air in your veins or arteries and also during surgery."

And with that, he asked me to get some rest and will be sending someone to draw some blood soon. Since my chest was still in pain, I asked the doctor about that, and he said, "Could be from the pressure from CPR, but we can send you down for an X-ray of your chest cavity to ensure that you don't have any broken bones."

"Sounds cool to me," I responded. The doctor left, and my sister asked if I was okay. And I said, "Kinda, it's a blessing to still be here." As I was lying in the gurney thinking to myself this was nothing but a dream. It had to be a dream. Ain't no way I'm really living this nightmare.

When will this situation become a reality to me as I watch the automatic blood pressure machine check my blood pressure, looking down at my arms, wondering why I have in both arms an IV needle. A nurse came into my room and drew my blood before they take me down to get my x-ray done. It looked like I will be staying here tonight. The only thing I can think of was how much I hate hospitals. I'm not used to being held captive and not being able to do what I want and go where I want while lying in this hospital gurney with tubes all in my arms and the sound of the machine monitoring my heart and pulse beeping constantly.

Finally, a nurse came and prepped me for the x-ray. I asked where she was taking me, and she said that she could do the x-ray right here. And she stepped out the room and came back in the room with a portable x-ray machine. By now, I nodded off briefly and was awakened by my sixteen-year-old son standing beside me with the look of terror in his eyes. My son said in a shaking voice, "Dad, are you okay?" His facial expression was priceless.

I said to him, "I guess I'm okay for the most part," which I knew I wasn't. I just didn't want him to be worrying himself about me while I'm in this hospital. I asked him, "Where is his sister at? Was she coming?"

And he said he doesn't know. I could truly understand if she doesn't. She was probably still upset with me for divorcing her mom and moving out.

While spending time with my son, my brother-in-law walked into my ICU room. He said that he found out what happened to me today and that he and my oldest sister, Valerie, came to see me. She was out in the waiting room talking to my sister, Kesha, and my wife, Yani. The doctors were only allowing two guests at a time to see me.

My son went to the waiting room to allow Valerie time to come see me. Val said that Kesha called her while she was at work and gave her a scare. She then called and told Willie what has happened.

After talking with Willie and Valerie for a little while, they told me good bye and left. My son, Kay, and my sister Kesha came into the room, and Kesha said it's starting to get late and her husband and kids were probably looking for their dinner and she would be back tomorrow to check on me. I said okay.

And she said, "I will take Kay home."

I said, "Okay, sis, thanks for everything." And with that being said, they left. Finally with all my visitors gone for today other than my wife, I was definitely in need of sleep with the day I just had and wanted to just close my eyes. I told my wife if she needed to, that she could go home tonight and just come back in the morning, and she refused to leave my side.

A nurse came into the room to give me some medicine and take my vitals, and I asked if I was getting a room soon. And she said that there aren't any rooms available due to overcrowding of the hospital and that I might get lucky tomorrow. The nurse also said that a tech would come and take me to get a MRI done also. My wife's phone started to ring, and she answered it and said, "Hi, Aunt Tia. Yeah, he's doing much better," and put her on speakerphone.

She said she pretty much understood what had happened to me and asked if I have given my life to God and repented for my sins. And I said no, and she said was I ready to do so now. And without hesitation, I said yes. And Aunt Tia and her husband, Jeff, began to pray for me. They asked the Lord to wash my sins in the blood of Jesus and to cleanse my soul from the crown of my head to the bottom of my feet. I can't explain it, but a feeling that I can't even begin to explain had come over me. I can feel it in my heart, and it was that moment that I was born again.

Thinking to myself, this is probably the reason that God had allowed me a second chance at life. Uncle Jeff advised if I didn't have an attorney that it would be a good thing to get one as soon as possible, and they prayed for a speedy recovery and gave their good night blessings. After nodding off, I was awakened by a tech to go and got the MRI of my neck around ten something that night. Once again, the tech pushed my gurney out the room and down the corridor toward the elevator. I had to pass through the horror movie scene with gurneys lined up against the wall with sick and in pain bodies filling them. What I would give to get out of this place. The feeling of anxiety just overpowered my thoughts.

The elevator doors opened up, and the tech pushed me out into the corridor and down a small ramp through some double fire doors and stopped just shy of a door on my right. Out came a guy, and he told the tech he got it from here and pushed me into the room and explained the procedure of the MRI and helped me onto the platform and got me situated and let me know it would take thirty minutes to complete the scan and gave me a remote to buzz if I needed to stop the scan for any reason and left me in the room to start the machine.

After my thirty minutes was up, the tech stopped the machine and helped me back into my gurney, and the tech came and led me back to the elevator and back passed the horror scene through the corridor back to my room in the ICU where my wife was asleep. Now that I was up, I was on Google looking at expensive $100,000 to $300,000 sports cars. It was just after 1:00 a.m., and a tech came in with a machine to do an echocardiogram of my heart and attached all of these leads to me, and about after ten minutes, he told my wife and I that my heart seemed fine and didn't show any signs of damage.

While the tech was removing the leads, a nurse came in to the room to check on me and to provide me with more medications. And I told her that I couldn't sleep, and she said that the medicine she was giving me should help me rest. After taking the pills, my wife wanted to pray before I went to sleep. Before this traumatic event happened, I wasn't a God-fearing man, but now since I have let Jesus into my heart and believed that he died for our sins, I now can say I'm a God-fearing man. So my wife and I prayed, and in no time, I was counting sheep.

You really don't get to sleep long in the hospital at all. Every two hours a nurse was coming to check my vitals and giving me medications. Well, I did live to see another day. I guess it's no reason to complain at all. I just barely escaped the grip of death if it wasn't for my God sparing my life that day. I'm blessed and thankful to still be alive. The reality still hadn't really hit me yet. It still felt like I was dreaming. After being awaken for the vital check, I couldn't go back to sleep, so I look at the time on my phone, and it was ten minutes past two. And I tried closing my eyes, but the anxiety of trying to sleep just started tearing away at me. The fear of not waking up was the reality I was facing now, so I just laid in the bed staring at the ceiling. And before you know it, another nurse walked in to check my vitals and gave me some more pills to take. That means it must be past 4:00 a.m. I looked at my phone for the time, and it was 4:05 a.m. on the dot.

Once again, I was just lying there on the gurney ready to get out of this place, giving all praises to God as I pray for the chest pains and headaches to go away, and I also prayed to go home. The routine didn't change. At 6:00 a.m. a nurse and medications. Also at 8:00 a.m., another nurse and medications. By this time, my wife was up and wanted to check on her son, who is my stepson, at home, and she left to go feed our son, Javon at 8:30 a.m. Then 10:00 a.m. rolled around, and once again, a nurse and more medications.

As noon approached, my wife came back to visit me, and she brought me a pair of pajamas to put on and she also brought my big fluffy light brown boot-looking slippers that my mother and father-in-law gifted me for Christmas. Aww, man, I love these comfortable slippers. My wife also gave me my charger since my iPhone 8 was on the verge of dying.

After twelve o'clock, a nurse rolled in to check my vitals and brought me medications to take and said, "The doctor will be coming to talk to you about discharge." And you know me, that was like music to my ears. While my wife and I were passing time away by talking about what happened to me, 6:00 p.m. rolled around quickly, and still no doctor had come to talk to me about a discharge. And the curtain swung open, and there were my little brothers from another mother, my true homies, Bud and Mikey.

Seeing them made my day. We kicked for a bit, and they talked about my cardiac arrest and how glad they were that I was still here.

Just hearing that made my eyes water up. Not long after, the curtain swung open again, and my uncle, Bookie, and my father, also named Kenny, walked in. And for me to see my father just eased my heart because I really don't see him much. I guess you can say that after getting older, my relationship with my dad has changed when I started my own family. Seeing him and my uncle just made me realize how important it is to keep close with your family because at any given moment, anything can happen that could change that.

I mean just think about it. We don't know when God will come and just take you away. The Bible states that in the rapture, Jesus comes like a thief in the night. And when he comes after this miracle I just witnessed, I want to be prepared and join him in the paradise of heaven for eternity.

The doctor walked in and handed my wife my discharge papers, shook my hand, and said, "Take it easy, Mr. Hough. You're a walking miracle," and left. As I was getting dressed, Bud heard a commotion outside of my room, so he took a peek and saw someone being brought into the ICU and appeared to be suffering from gunshot wounds.

He said, "Hey, fool, man slim got hit up!"

And Mikey took a peek and said, "Hey, that's tough." And I wasn't concerned with that. I was trying to get out of this place, and at that moment, a lady doctor came and told Bud and Mikey that they couldn't do that and it was an emergency situation and they couldn't be out of the room and we couldn't come out until they take care of the situation. Just hearing the ER doctors working on trying to save that man's life sounded like a skit from a movie. All our faces dropped when the man succumbed to his injuries. Minutes later, the lady doctor came to the room and said that we may now leave.

To be headed home was all I wanted. There's no feeling like being able to lie in your own bed. My wife wouldn't allow me to do nothing for myself. She was treating me like a king. I guess I couldn't complain, but the only thing was that she had been treating me like a king. The pain in my chest still hurt, and these headaches were still killing me. The pain wasn't letting up at all. I felt fragile now. My voice was still damaged. I'm guessing from the CPR. I still didn't know what happened to me other than that I had a cardiac arrest.

Curiosity started to get the best of me, so I asked my wife if I could see my discharge papers. After looking through the papers, and I saw the cause of the cardiac arrest was allergic reaction to lidocaine. After reading that and thinking to myself for a few minutes, I started to question it. How could I be allergic to lidocaine after all of this? I mean, come on. I have had many dentist appointments in the past from the time I had to get cavities filled as a kid to getting wisdom teeth and a molar pulled as an adult, and lidocaine was used each time. Also I had been to the outpatient place four times prior before the cardiac arrest, and nothing happened. So how did I have a cardiac arrest now? This question will be planted into the back of my head until I find out what really happened to me. I know for a fact that someone was trying to sweep this under the rug like it never happened, and I had a drive and love to research information to find what I'm looking for and adamant about it.

After a day of turmoil, dealing with these headaches that the doctors called spinal headaches, and these chest pains were not letting up also. It was killing my wife to see me in so much agony. She said, "We are going back to the hospital if your pains continue." Well, as you know the pains never let up, so my wife helped me get dressed and back to hospital number two in Washington, DC. We arrived there by 11:00 a.m. on February 18, 2019, and they took my vitals and had us waiting in the waiting room forever. Finally, someone came back to get me and took me back to get a CT scan of my head and told me to have a seat outside a pair of double doors. If I knew this hospital was going to be still overcrowded after my last visit, I would have asked my wife to take me to a different hospital.

I couldn't keep my eyes open much longer and nodded off. Someone came and awakened me and finally took me into the back to get the CT scan done and walked me back out to the waiting room. After a while, a doctor came out and told my wife and I that the scan doesn't show anything abnormal and there was still a little air on my brain and it should dissipate within a couple of days. As far as the headaches go, they are called spinal headaches and should be gone within a week.

I asked, "What about my chest pains, Doc?"

And the doctor responded with, "They are most likely from the CPR and should go away in a week or two."

I looked at my wife and gave her a look of disappointment as I frowned and said, "Can you please take me home?"

And she said, "Awe, baby, it will be okay. I know you're going through a lot. God will take away the pain."

We didn't get out of there until 4:30 p.m., and I wasn't even hungry. But of course, you know my wife would not let me go about not eating. We stopped at Subway, and she got a tuna sub, and she got me half a roast beef sub with swiss cheese. And we went home. I tried everything possible to kill these headaches, and nothing seemed to work as the day turned into night. And my wife took some days off from work to stay home with me since she was now my care provider. We started to pray together every night ever since my cardiac arrest. She always prayed even before my accident. I'm the one that didn't, and trust me, I felt a lot of guilt behind it.

I tried my best to fall asleep, but for some reason, I just couldn't. No matter how hard I tried, I just couldn't seem to sleep. So I started digging into researching cardiac arrest, cardiac arrest statistics, and cardiac arrest survivors. When I say I'm blessed to be alive, trust me, I really mean it. Just seeing these statistics of survivors made me cry. Reading from a site I googled on the subject, it stated that there is more than 356,000 out of hospital cardiac arrests annually just in the US alone, and 90 percent of them are fatal. That's nearly a thousand people a day, and only 10 percent are making it out the hospital for discharge. I couldn't hold back the tears any longer, and my wife heard me and begged that I stop and go to sleep.

The next day, I was starting to know that I was having more complications going on with my body. I feel off. Not only was I dealing with the chest pains and headaches, but now I was experiencing numbness on the right side of my body, loss of balance while trying to walk, and muscle pains across my stomach and bladder. While on bed rest per doctor's orders, I spent my time researching more about epidural injections and how they relate to cardiac arrest, and allergic reactions to lidocaine also. I was not giving up this research until I find out what happened to me.

This was another day of experiencing agonizing headaches and chest pains. I got a call from my company's risk management nurse, and she asked me how I was feeling. And I explained my pains, and she suggested I go to the ER and to not take this lightly. Trying my best to man up and fight through the pains, I managed to make through another day. But Wifey insisted that we are going to the hospital tomorrow morning. And for me to hear the word *hospital*, I threw a temper tantrum like a little kid that couldn't get a toy from the toy store.

I told my wife if I got to go, we should try another hospital and to please not take me back to hospital number two. She agreed also. Since digging into my research deeper, insomnia wasn't the only thing kicking my behind. I had a fear of going to sleep now thinking I would die in my sleep from another cardiac arrest. So as you know, I got back into my research, finally able to close my eyes just before the crack of dawn.

The date was February 21, 2019, and my wife and I headed toward hospital number 3, which was in DC also. And we had to park in a garage across the street and walk about the length of a block to get there. Now that I was having balancing issues, my wife had to help me walk by allowing me to lean on her while walking. Once inside of the hospital, we stopped to talk to a security guard about how do we get to the ER. And she told us that the emergency room was packed to capacity and would be a two- to four-hour wait and said, "How you been, Kenny?"

And I know who she was, but for the love of me, I can't remember her name at all. So I responded, "Not so good right now. I just survived a cardiac arrest a couple of days ago," and introduced my wife to her. She couldn't believe it and told me to take it easy and it was nice seeing me. We decided to not wait and headed back to the car.

The sky has now turned pitch-black, and a storm was right on top of us. As we made it to the car, I told my wife that I know the security guard. We went to school together, and she had come out to support my band that I have played with also definitely a good friend. My wife then decided to get me out of DC and wanted to take me to the state of Virginia to one of their hospitals. I was against it at first but then agreed to it.

It was rush hour in pouring down rain, but we managed to get to hospital number four in approximately forty-five minutes, which wasn't bad at all. We walked right into the hospital ER and talked to the clerical staff to get signed in after stating my reason for coming. And in no time, we were already being called back for vitals and given a room and a gown to put on. Minutes later, a nurse came in and inserted my IV and took some blood and told me a doctor would be with me shortly. My wife and I watched some television for a little while, and the doctor walked in and asked a few questions concerning what brought me to the hospital and why.

After getting the answers he needed, he instructed the technician, and I was off to get another CT head scan, chest scan, ECG with twelve leads for my heart, and an MRI C-spine without contrast. My blood pressure was 130/73, pulse 71, and weighed in at 161 pounds. After getting all of that done in a timely manner, while discussing with my wife how fast and efficient this hospital was and how much I liked this one, I said, "We should have came here first."

At that moment, the doctor walked in and said, "It's amazing that you are still walking! Your injury to your cervical spine has really damaged your spinal cord, and you need an emergency spinal surgery ASAP! If you don't get this corrected immediately, this could result to paralysis of your extremities!"

Just to hear the word *surgery* gave me some form of anxiety, and I told the doctor, "No, sir. We are not doing any surgeries, buddy. You can go ahead and bring us those discharge papers."

Never seen a doctor get mad before, but this one was pissed. He walked out the room with an attitude. I asked my wife, "What's wrong with him?" And she just gave me a look of shock. The nurse came in with my discharge papers, and we left to go home.

After getting home a little before 2:00 p.m., I called my elevator union to let them know that I went to the hospital today but discharged myself because they were going to send me to another hospital to get surgery and I got scared and feared dying again. And they said that I couldn't discharge myself for insurance purposes for worker's comp to cover the cost and that I need to go back. And at that moment, I just broke down crying and said okay and got off the phone.

My union must have called my attorney because my phone started ringing, and it was him. And he said, "Kenny, you have to go back, buddy." And in a crying voice, I tried to tell him that they were going to kill me and I didn't want to die.

"Please, I'm not ready to die!"

After he convinced me that I needed to go, I said okay and got off the phone and my son, Kay, heard a slight commotion and came into my room and said, "What's wrong, Dad?"

And I said, "I gotta go back to the hospital to get surgery on my spine," and broke out crying all over again. He started crying also for about five minutes. I had to ask God for the strength to pull us together, and he answered. I stopped crying and told my son that everything was going to be alright. God wasn't going to let me die again. We got to just trust and believe in him.

Now that was the strength I needed, and I called my wife to let her know that I need to talk to her when she got in. She had to go pick up my stepson, Jay, from basketball practice. And when she got in, I told her what was going on and what my attorney had said, and of course, she was against it, but she said, "Well, baby, if that's the case, we will just pray and put it in God's hands, baby." With a strong look of confidence, she said, "I'm ready whenever you are ready, baby."

We told the boys what was going on, and they wanted to ride with us. And we all left, got in the car, and our destination was hospital number five out Virginia, the one that hospital four wanted to transport me to for surgery. After arriving at the hospital, I checked in and told the clerk why I came to be seen and handed over my discharge papers. After verifying everything, they took me back into the ER, got me in a gown, and took my vitals, some blood, and urine and had me in a gurney waiting for a doctor to come and talk to me.

My in-laws, Tawana and Steve, called my wife and let her know that they were forty minutes away from being in the area. They were coming up from South Carolina to visit me and to also help out any way they can. Since the doctors wouldn't let our boys back into the ER due to the fact the emergency room was full to capacity, my wife decided to take them home and to greet her parents when they arrived.

Twenty minutes had gone by, and a nurse came to take me to a room finally. The room had two beds, a bathroom, and I had a roommate. He had his curtain up, talking to his visitors, so I couldn't see him at the time. I just lay back and waited for Yani to call me to let me know she was on her way back.

After nodding off, my iPhone was ringing and broke my sleep. I answered, and Yani said, "I'm on my way, baby. Do you want anything to eat?"

And I said, "No, baby, I'm good." A nurse came in and introduced herself and wrote my room number and nurse on duty that will be monitoring me on her shift. She also wrote the head doctor in charge of my floor and left. By this time, Yani made it back to the hospital and asked the front desk what room they were keeping me in. She walked in the room, and my roommate was headed to the bathroom. And he said hello and went inside the bathroom and closed the door. Yani pulled up a chair and put it beside the head of my bed.

My roommate came out and formally introduced himself to us. He was a tall middle-aged White man with gray hair. He was walking back to his bed while pushing some tall metal stand that was holding bags of fluid with hoses attached to it and the other side attached to him. He seemed like a nice guy. He talked to us for a good while, and he was in due to a blood transfusion and was waiting on his blood to be at a certain level so he can go home.

I told him that I was here for a surgery of my spine. While giving him details of why I need surgery, a doctor came in and introduced himself as a neurosurgeon. And he said that he would be the one doing the surgery on me tomorrow morning. He asked me a couple of questions about how I got the injury before the cardiac arrest and why I discharged myself instead of letting the ambulance bring me. After telling him, I also told him I didn't want to die, and at that moment, it came to me. It had to be God.

Out of nowhere, I asked to see a cardiologist. I asked the doctor, "What about my heart? I just had a cardiac arrest." I said, "My heart couldn't handle the strain of being put under for a couple of hours for a surgery."

The doctor said, "Okay, I will get you a cardiologist and set you up for an echocardiogram."

And he left out, and the first thing my wife said, "That was some smart thinking right there, baby, to buy you some time to make sure your heart is good."

And I said, "I know, right? But it wasn't me."

And she put her arms around me and said, "Thank you, Jesus." My mother-in-law, Tawana, but I call her Ma, had called Yani and her and my father-in-law, Steve, whom I called Dad, was on speakerphone talking to us and asked how I was doing. And they prayed with us, and Yani told them I bought us some time by asking to see a cardiologist to clear me for surgery.

They said, "That was a smart move, son."

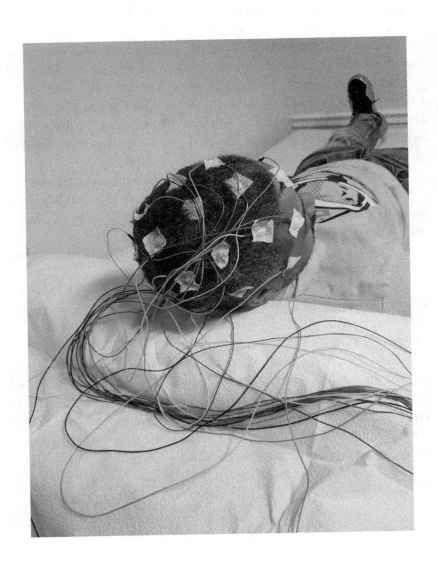

No word from the cardiologist as the night came and went, and I wasn't planning on being in this hospital any longer than expected. During the night, I had to deal with the nurse on duty checking up on me and giving me medications to take to help me with the pains I was dealing with. The night had turned to morning quick, and time started flying. Some more of my family came to visit me after finding out about my emergency surgery. My great-uncle, Randy, and his wife, Great-Aunt Ann, came to visit me. Randy now was a minister for the Lord, and I took Uncle Randy's presence as a sign from God.

I hadn't seen Uncle Randy in a while, and it felt good to see him. He prayed for me, and not just for me, he also ministered the Word of God to my roommate. And my roommate was so full of joy that you could see it in his face.

He said, "No stranger has ever prayed for me before."

And Uncle Randy said, "I'm no stranger but a brother from God."

After Uncle Randy and Aunt Ann left, my sister, Kesha, and her husband, Seven, came to visit me also with their three children who are young teenagers: little Seven, Najee, and Zye. My father, Kenny, and Uncle Bookie even came to see me again. Everyone was against the surgery in fear of the what if factor if things don't go right.

After visitation was over, my wife went home and was coming back in the morning. And she said she would call me when she got in and still no sign of the cardiologist. And I asked the nurse on duty when I was seeing him, and her response was she wasn't sure but she would ask someone for me. And I said, "Okay. Thank you so much," and watched a little bit of television as the night got late. My wife called, and we talked for a good while before she insisted I try to get some sleep. For some reason, I just couldn't sleep. I didn't want to close my eyes. I tried but had too much on my mind. The fear of getting surgery was heavily on my mind.

When I finally fell asleep, my roommate and I were awaken three something in the morning by a patient down the hall screaming and yelling. He literally woke the whole floor up. About twenty minutes later, the nurses finally calmed down the out-of-control patient. There wasn't any use of going back to sleep. The nurse was due to do her rounds at four, so I just stayed up until then. After the usual routine with the vitals check and the administering of medications, I drifted to sleep.

Morning came, and my wife called to see if I needed anything from home before she left. When my wife arrived, she ordered my breakfast from the cafeteria, and my roommate and I told her about the screaming patient. And she couldn't believe it. Before noon, my roommate got good news from his doctor that he was being discharged, and by 2:00 p.m., his wife came to get him. And they said bye and wished me luck and also said that my great-uncle was a great guy. Yani and I kicked it a bit as we bonded more and her cousin, Kim's husband, Ken, called Yani and said that he was in the area and if I needed or wanted anything. And I had a taste for a roast beef sub from Subway and in thirty minutes flat, Cousin Ken delivered.

It felt good to see that my extended family cared and worried for my health. Cousin Ken talked to us for a while before he had to leave. My Cousin Chauncey found out through my sister, and he even came to see me. It had been a while since I last saw him. We have so many memories together. My Uncle Joe is his grandfather, and he took my sister and myself in my junior year of high school when I got in trouble with the law and was having problems with my mom. He got to meet Yani for the first time and didn't even know that I was married. After spending time with Chauncey, he left and my oldest sister, Valerie, and her husband, Willie, my brother-in-law, paid me a visit also.

I was having a good day until night came and all my visitors left and I still haven't seen the cardiologist yet. Yani decided to stay with me tonight, and once again, I couldn't sleep. I just couldn't close my eyes and don't know why. I just couldn't close them. Before you know it, someone started screaming again around the coincidental time of three something in the morning, and it scared Yani as she was awakened. I chuckled and said, "Right on schedule." Morning came, and here it was Sunday, and I was still here. This is definitely not what I had planned. The frustration started to kick in. Yani ordered my breakfast to get the day started.

Before breakfast came, a nurse came and said that the cardiologist would be here this morning to see me, and I said, "Now that's good news to my ears." The nurse took me out into the hallway by means of a wheelchair and down a corridor to do a balancing and walking exercise. I didn't even have the idea that something was wrong with me balancing and walking until now. I couldn't keep my balance as I kept leaning too far to the right, the same side that I have all the numbness and nerve pains. The nurse took me back to my room and said that I will need a cane and gave me one.

By this time, my breakfast was back, so my wife and I ate, and finally, the cardiologist arrive. Talking about perfect timing, seeing him just made all the nervousness escalate. He introduced himself and shook my hand, and said, "I never shook the hand of a ghost before. You shouldn't be here after what happened to you." He said that I was a lucky man and that my echocardiogram shows that my heart wasn't ready for a two- to four-hour surgery. Man, that was music to my ears as my wife and I gave all prayers to God. Yani was so excited that she called Mom and Dad and told them the good news while I gathered my belongings so I can be discharged and get up out of this place. Yani helped dress me, and we were headed home.

After arriving at home, the first thing I did was jump into the shower. I noticed while in the shower, I had to hold my balance against the wall to keep from falling over. Now this was definitely something new. *What is going on with my body?* I asked myself. After finishing my shower, I had a little trouble dressing myself, and Yani kept insisting she help. But I was so used to doing things on my own that I wouldn't allow her to help me. I kept telling myself I got this and that there was nothing wrong with me.

I texted my company's risk management nurse to let her know that I was finally home from the hospital, and she recommended me to stay on bed rest until March 12, 2019. I was just anxious on going back to work and getting back into the swing of things. I definitely wasn't planning on being out of work this long. I was not used to just lying around. I had been a go-getter ever since I can remember. I had been grinding ever since I was twelve years old doing two paper routes before school, starting my mornings at 3:30 a.m. to get money.

As we start the weekday off, my wife took off some time from work to be my care giver to help me around the house. Still I wouldn't let her help me the way she wanted to. I was embarrassed to not be able to do for myself. But Yani would not give up being there for me. That morning I got a call from my attorney, and I told him that I wasn't cleared for surgery. He recommended me to see an orthopedic surgeon that he knew and gave me his number to call.

I called the surgeon, and he scheduled me an appointment to see him on March 6, 2019. A week went by, and I started paying more attention to my body. I was noticing more things that I was not used to doing that I was doing now. I was being very forgetful, putting stuff in the fridge that went in the cabinet and vice versa. I was having a hard time remembering words that I used to say while having a conversation. I was stuttering while talking, forgetting names of friends, and the list seemed like it went on and on.

This new scenario was starting to scare me and had me thinking that I suffered more than just a cardiac arrest. I thought I was suffering from other injuries related to this also. As the days went by, my headaches were not letting up at all. They were extensive and damaging and lasted all day and night.

March 4, 2019, I emailed the worker's compensation adjuster informing her that I did not receive my pay for week ending February, 27, 2019, and I let my supervisor know. And he said that he would look into it. My main concern for my pay was that I did not want to be in noncompliance for child support. I rarely miss work, and this was out of my hands. Hours later, my supervisor contacted me to let me know that they will pay me for that week, and I sent a disregard email.

Later on the adjuster responded back and said, "In the future, all questions such as these should be directed to your attorney's office as I'm not allowed to contact you directly per their rules. I just didn't want you to think I never received your email at all though." Wow, I didn't know it was rules of engagement when it came to this matter I was dealing with. At that moment, it felt like someone was chopping my brain with an ax the way these excruciating headaches were attacking me.

I tried to mask the pain and just smiled, but with these headaches, you can't hide the pain. Every time Yani saw my face and knew that I was being tormented from these headaches that the doctors called spinal headaches, she just cried and wished she could take them away from me. She would lay her hands on my head and pray for me, and tears would just roll out the corners of my eyes. The morning of March 6, I arrived mid-morning for my appointment in the city of DC to see the orthopedic surgeon. After he looked at my MRI, he told me about a surgery that could possibly help my condition. The surgeon told me about anterior cervical discectomy and fusion with metal plating applied to the C5 to C7 spine.

He said that he would make an incision just below my throat to remove the disc and put in bone graft and secure the vertebrae with a metal plate and showed me x-rays of patients that had the procedure done. He recommended surgery be done in a hospital setting just in case anything was to go wrong that he had everything he needs. I told him that I would think about it and let him know, and he said he would email me a packet to fill out when I'm ready. He also wrote me a letter to give to my employer to remain home from work indefinitely.

After leaving the surgeon's office and explaining the required surgery to Yani, she was already against it. Yani wanted me to get a second opinion. She really didn't believe surgery was the best option for me. She wanted me to see another doctor before I decide to do the surgery. I was so used to making decisions on my own that I wasn't thinking about us. I was being selfish and was thinking about me. I was the one that had a cardiac arrest. I was the one that had severe headaches. I was the one that could barely talk. I was the one with severe chest pains. I was the one that got to walk with a cane, and I was the one that had chronic nerve pain. I totally forgot that we were one and this had been a traumatic experience for her also.

On March 8, 2020, I let my employer nurse case manager that my benefits form for me to continue getting union benefits was filled out by the orthopedic surgeon and had me out of work from February 15 until TBD pending surgery limitations, pain, and weakness.

I just want the pains to stop and my normal life back, so I responded to the surgeon's email on March 12, 2019 without Yani's consent. The surgeon's assistant responded back immediately with a packet that I need to fill out with all the information I needed to know about the surgery and the date of the surgery, which was scheduled for April 2, 2019. I didn't want to tell her, but I couldn't keep this from her so I told her. And of course, she was pissed and called Aunt Tia later on that evening so she could tell me her experiences after getting the same surgery that I need done.

After listening to Aunt Tia's testimony and all the pain she still was going through to this day after her surgery, I was still not sold. I just wanted it to be over. I was not even having any fears of the possible outcomes this surgery could have. It seemed my decision was tearing Yani and myself up. Yani already lost her grandmother on her mother's side of the family in the last quarter of 2018 and her Uncle Boe in January of 2019 and feared losing me to this surgery. After a few days, I started to notice more changes within my body. Not only was I having weakness and numbness on the right side of my body, now I was experiencing blurry vision that came and went, slurred speech, stuttering, forgetting words while trying to hold a conversation, muscle spasms, pains in my neck, numbness in both feet, problems holding my bladder, incontinence, muscle pains across my stomach and bladder and right side rib cage and shoulder that were causing a burning sensation and numb feeling, chest and upper back pains along with these severe headaches.

I'm spending nights on end depriving myself of sleep on Google researching my symptoms because I know it was more that happened to my body from the cardiac arrest. These complications got to be from more damage that was caused, but I just didn't know exactly, but I would definitely find out. As the days and nights started to slowly pass me by, I started digging into cardiac arrest, resuscitation, and symptoms, and came across three names: hypoxia, global cerebral ischemia, and reperfusion injury.

Hypoxia is a partial lack of oxygen to the brain, and global cerebral ischemia is the lack of blood flow to the entire brain after three minutes, and I was told I was out of there for eight minutes. Symptoms are severe memory loss, involuntary muscle contractions, loss of muscle control, loss of mobility, and fine motor control and urine and bladder problems. And reperfusion injury is the sudden rush of blood to areas of damaged tissues. The absence of oxygen and nutrients during the blood deprived period creates a situation in which the restoration of blood flow places oxidative stress on the brain as pooled toxins flood already damaged tissues and can trigger a cascade of symptoms from mild to severe including severe head-aches, seizures, weakness or paralysis on one side of the body, vision loss or blindness in one eye, difficulty comprehending things heard or spoken, loss of awareness and attention in environment, slurred or jumbled speech, dizziness or vertigo, double vision, and loss of coordination at times.

After reading all of this, it automatically had me thinking that I suffered some form of a minor stroke. I was having some of these same symptoms. Thinking I found my problem, how do I go about getting the help I need to see the right doctors?

I first let Yani know what I thought had happened to me, and by her being a God-fearing woman, first thing she said, "Well, how do you know? You're not a doctor. You shouldn't speak negative on your situation. You need to claim you're healed in the name of Jesus!"

"Yes, you're absolutely right," I said.

"Can you please get a second opinion about the surgery?" she asked.

And I responded with, "For you, of course."

As the days passed by, I found myself going into a state of depression and feared going to sleep due to the fact that I kept try-ing to find more information about my complications and what was really the cause of my cardiac arrest. I needed someone to talk to concerning my self-diagnosis other than Yani, someone who I could rationalize with, someone who researched to keep me on my toes also, and that person was my sister, Kesha. I knew if I told her what I was experiencing as far as my symptoms were concerned, she would get on top of it and let me know what I had to do.

I told Kesha about the surgery I had to get, and she asked me if I was going to go through with it. And I told her yes, and she said I shouldn't do it and if I thought this out before agreeing to the surgery and what the success rate of the procedure was. I told her that I didn't know. I did not read any of the paperwork that was emailed to me. Kesha said to read the paperwork and let her know what it said. And I said okay. I went back to look at my papers and not once did I read any of this! I can't believe I signed and initialed these forms without reading any of it!

On the second page, it stated that it was important that I was aware of the risks and that I was sure I was doing the right thing. As I started reading through the rest of the papers, on the fifth page it said that it had been explained to me and I fully understood that there were certain risks associated with this procedure. The risk included, among other things, death, permanent full paralysis, permanent partial paralysis, voice box paralysis in anterior cervical surgery, permanent brain damage, permanent partial blindness, permanent complete blindness, infection, bowel and or bladder dysfunction, visceral or vascular injury, neural or dural injury, stroke, heart attack, further corrective surgery, blood transfusion problems, and temporary or permanent severe pains. And I initialed this without even reading it first. I initialed more on the next page, and I did not want to read any more of it. I called Kesha and told her what the papers said and she said, "Bro, don't get that surgery!"

And I said, "I don't want to. Trust me."

I noticed just sitting around in the house that my feet were still getting cold and numb. Just trying to play games on my Xbox One, my arms and hands would become numb and just burn badly to a point I no longer wanted to play my games. My conditions and symptoms weren't getting any better either. Wednesday, March 20, 2019, being on bed rest is for the birds. Watching the idiot box, which my great grandmother used to call the television, rest her soul, was killing me. I mean that I was accustomed to waking up every morning at four and turning wrenches at 6:00 a.m., the life of an elevator mechanic to be productive.

There's no productivity just lying in the bed by yourself. When Yani got home from work later that evening, we started researching on how to eat healthy and wrote an extensive list out. Friday, March 22, I did Yani's taxes for her to save her from paying someone to do them for her. Sunday, March 24, 2019, Yani and I researched the benefits of lemon water to see if it would help with any of my symptoms. That night we discussed the surgery once again, and she wanted me to get a second opinion. And after reading through those papers previously, I finally agreed that it was the best decision for me to listen to her.

Wednesday, March 27, 2019, around noon, I got a call from my attorney, and he wanted some brief information from me about my cardiac arrest and what was being done to treat me. Also I talked to my company's risk management nurse, and she was working on getting authorization for me to see a neurologist and a cardiologist for surgery clearance. Monday, March 29, 2019, I got a call from someone from a hospital in Washington, DC, regarding my surgery on April 2 to confirm my arrival time and what I must do to prepare for the surgery. I let her know that the surgery was on hold until I get cleared by a cardiologist. Sunday, April 1, 2019, I was still dealing with unexplainable pains, and the lack of sleep wasn't making it any better.

Staying up from sundown to sunup with fears of dying kept playing tricks on my mind. That night dealing with these ongoing nerve pains and severe headaches, Yani asked me to get in touch with my risk management nurse and push for my authorizations. Yani knew when I get frustrated. This whole ordeal has been one frustrated situation. Yani said that she would fall back some and let me deal with my situation the way I need to.

April 3, 2019, I emailed my employer case nurse and told her that the neurologist wanted someone to authorize and schedule my appointment. And she said someone would be calling me to schedule. Finally, I got my appointment scheduled with neurologist. And on Tuesday, April 9, 2019, I went to see the neurologist, and I didn't bring any paperwork with me, but I told him my symptoms and problems and told him I think I suffered some type of trauma to my brain due to lack of oxygen. He agreed to do an EEG test of my brain and scheduled me an appointment for the twenty-fifth of April.

My risk management nurse got my clearance to see a cardiologist that my wife picked for me to see. Thursday, April 11, 2019, I was researching transient ischemic attacks at 7:54 p.m. and discussed this with Yani. And she didn't agree that I was suffering from any of those symptoms. Wednesday night, April 15, 2019, I was suffering from severe headaches and blurred vision, and Yani took me back to hospital number four in the state of Virginia. After they took my vitals, which my blood pressure was 131/65 and pulse was 53, weighing 153 lbs. They got me into a bay in the emergency room and put something in my IV line that put me out.

After waking up from my sleep, I was discharged and diagnosed with a headache disorder and given a prescription for butalbital-acetaminophen-caffeine pills. On Friday, April 17, 2019, I had my appointment with the cardiologist, and he asked me why I was there and a few other small questions. He also got some blood samples from me and some sonogram pictures of my heart. After seeing the results of the sonogram, he said that my heart wasn't ready for any surgery at this time. He said my heart shows a lot of damage on the walls of my lower left ventricle, and he prescribed me some pills called carvedilol to slow my heart down so it won't have to work as hard or fast to pump blood.

After leaving the cardiologist office, I went to CVS to put my prescription in and purchased a blood pressure monitor. While waiting on my prescription, I researched what carvedilol was for and Google said, "It's a beta blocker that can treat high blood pressure, heart failure, and reduce the risk of death after a heart attack."

Thursday, April 25, 2019, Yani took off from work to take me to get the EEG test done, which is short for *electroencephalogram* and is used to find problems related to electrical activities of the brain. The tech explained the test to Yani and I and had me lay down on the gurney, and he put these colorful electrodes all over my head and started the test. When the test was done, the tech explained that the neurologist would go over the test results with me and sent us to the waiting room.

About thirty minutes later, they called us back to talk with the neurologist, and this time I didn't forget any of my paperwork, hospital discharges, MRI, etc. The neurologist said that my results were negative and showed no signs of any damage done. So I asked, "Well, what is causing me all these problems I'm dealing with? What is causing these painful headaches? Something is wrong with me and I know it!"

And again he said, "I recommend you get surgery, but don't get surgery."

And I repeated, "So you saying to get the surgery but don't get the surgery?" And he nodded his head, and I looked at Yani. Her facial expression was like she was confused with what the neurologist said, like her face was saying WHAT? I told her to come on. I heard enough of this dude. I don't think he knew what he was talking about. This didn't even make any since at all.

Friday, April 26, 2019, my employer nurse case manager reached out to me to get my attorney's email address to cancel the conference call due to laryngitis. She also emailed him for his thoughts moving forward. She told me that the neurologist's notes from my visit wasn't ready yet. I said, "The neurologist wasn't very helpful." And she said that she knew and was sorry. At that moment, something came over me, and I had a mental breakdown. And I told her I just want my old body back and started to cry. She said, "She understands and will do all she can to help." I refused to accept my condition, and I wanted answers, so I spent the rest of my day researching peripheral neuropathy and its causes, symptoms, and treatments.

I know for a fact now that I have nerve damage and a damaged heart also, but what else is damaged in my body that I don't know about? as I asked myself. Now my time was being consumed by my research. I was determined to find out what was wrong with me. I was afraid to die. Another night of not getting any sleep had Yani worried about my well-being. April 30, 2019, the worker's compensation RN field case manager texted me at 1:33 p.m. and said:

Hey, so I'm on a road today but give me a
brief summary of what the neurologist said and

when is your next appointment? Hope you're doing well. I'm headed to Baltimore.

I said, "He said that the EEG doesn't show anything."

I asked him for a copy and he said, "Why? Your insurance company can get the results." I asked him what was causing my complications and he said, "I'm not sure. Go and see a spine doctor. I don't recommend surgery, but get surgery." That threw my wife and me for a loop.

She said, "Oh, Jesus! Not much help."

And I said, "No." She asked when my next appointment was, and I told her May 20 with the cardiologist.

She said, "Perfect. Sorry, I'm rushing. When I get home, I will email the insurance company. Also the medication for your headaches was denied but gave no reason why."

I told her that they authorized my medication, and she said, "They told me it wouldn't be, and I was pissed. But okay. Well, forget I said that then."

Now remind you that this was the same lady that came to the hospital for the cardiac arrest death of me to retrieve the paperwork. May 1, 2019, I emailed my employer nurse case manager to let her know that the neurologist updated the information in the online app. Wednesday, May 8, 2019, I had an appointment with my primary care physician to keep him up-to-date with what was going on with me. After my appointment, I checked to see if my direct deposit posted to my account, and there was nothing there. I talked to my supervisor, and he directed me to contact someone from worker's compensation because they were paying me now from here on out.

I called my employer nurse case manager, and she directed me to call the worker's comp adjuster. I told her that I was not supposed to contact her, and she said, "Have your attorney contact her? I don't want to give you the wrong information." I asked her was authorization given for me to see the spine specialist and that I was really falling apart mentally. I couldn't wait weeks for appointments. I wanted help now before it's too late and new complications reveal itself. Some days I just wanted to cry.

And she said, "I'm working on the authorization to see the spine specialist. I know this is difficult for you. No, crying won't help. Stay tough. This is only temporary. We will get you on the right path soon. I will keep in touch."

May 13, 2019, I got a letter from the neurologist, and it read:

> Dear Mr. Hough, I find it necessary to inform you that as of May 9, 2019, I will no longer be able to serve as your neurologist. Unfortunately, your symptoms are out of my expertise. I strongly recommend you see your pain management doctor to continue treatment. I will continue to provide emergency medical care for only thirty days from the date of this letter. My office will send copies of your medical records regarding the care we have provided for you once we receive a written request from you granting us permission to do so.

I emailed my employer case nurse and sent her a copy of it. Can you believe this here? Thinking to myself that this man called himself a neurologist and couldn't help me! As days started passing me by, I've been consumed with thoughts during the nights of death due to my cardiac arrest and complications, making it hard for me to sleep due to these fears. They haunted me every night like ghosts in a bad dream.

Monday, May 20, 2019, I had an appointment with my cardiologist, and I texted my employer nurse case manager to let her know that my heart was showing signs of improvement. And the cardiologist gave me another prescription to fill. She said, "Omg. That's great news. Are you feeling better?" I told her I would go back for blood work June 6 and got to wear a portable heart monitor again and June 24, I had a follow-up appointment. They have me scheduled to see a different neurologist June 1. It told her that no, I was not feeling any better. The headaches were back.

On Wednesday, May 29, 2019, at 10:49 p.m., I got a text from the worker's comp RN medical field case manager, and she said, "How are you doing? Any new updates?" I told her that I was hanging in there. Nothing had changed as far as my pains and symptoms. My cardiologist did say my heart was improving and June 1 I was go to Baltimore to see another neurologist.

And she replied, "Wonderful. What time? I would love to go to that one if I can. Let me check my calendar to see if I can go to that if I can go. What is the neurologist's name and address?" I gave her all the information she needed, and her reply was, "Awesome. Thank you. Perfect."

Anxiety kicked in during the anticipation on waiting for the first to see this new neurologist and hoping that he or she could help me and answer these many questions I have about what happened to me.

The morning had finally fell upon Yani and I as we got up on this Saturday, June 1, 2019, to make this forty-five minute drive to Baltimore, Maryland, to hospital number seven to see my second neurologist to get some answers to what was going on with my body and to get the help I need. We found our way through the hospital to the doctor's office and signed in. While sitting and waiting to get called to the back, I was hoping that this worker's compensation nurse won't show up. I had one person ahead of me, and in no time, I was called to the back.

The neurologist greeted Yani and I and asked a few questions like, full name, date of birth, height, weight, and why I was there. After giving him this information, he asked why I was walking with a cane? I told him because my balance was off and while I was walking, I tend to lean too far to one side, resulting in falling over. He asked me to turn my head left and right far as I could and up and down as far as I could, and I complied. He asked if I saw a neurologist for my condition, and I said yes. And he asked well why didn't the neurologist help me. I told him that he said that my injury was beyond his expertise. He asked me if I drove, and I was starting to feel like I was not here for help. But I answer his question and said yes, sometimes I did but not far distances.

And at that moment, he jotted down some notes and recommended that I get surgery and said "good luck" and thanked us for coming. Now I'm confused and looked at Yani with a strange look upon my face and asked the neurologist, "Aren't you going to help me? Isn't that the reason I came to see you for?"

And he said, "You're here for insurance purposes only. Didn't your adjuster tell you that you are here for an assessment only? I would love to be your doctor and help you any way I can if they give authorization. Take care."

You talking about being highly upset. I couldn't believe we got up early on a Saturday morning to drive out to Baltimore just for an insurance assessment. I felt like a damaged car that had just been seen by a claim adjuster! I immediately texted my worker's compensation RN field case manager at 12:04 p.m. and said, "Hey, can you give me a call?" And it went unanswered. As Yani and I made our way back to the car, I took a second to talk to the Lord and asked why I came out here just to be turned away and received any help? Why, Lord, why?

And at that moment, a peace came upon me out of nowhere that softened my heart and removed the anger and cleared my thoughts so good that I asked Yani, "Why don't we just take a ride down to the Baltimore Harbor and enjoy the rest of this nice Saturday afternoon? No need on letting that doctor ruin the rest of our day."

So we drove down to the harbor, found a parking garage to park in, and we walked up and down along the harbor, took some pics and selfies by the water, stopped and got some ice cream from one of the vendors. We also went in a few stores, and as the evening approached, we headed on back home. I texted my employer nurse case manager and let her know that I went to Baltimore to see the neurologist, and it didn't go as I thought it should go. She asked what happened. And I told her that he asked me a few questions and afterward he said that I was only there for insurance purposes, so no treatment or nothing.

She asked, "Did he have an option regarding further treatment?"

And I told her, "He said that I should see a neurologist and good luck, and oh, and why didn't my last neurologist help me? I talked to my attorney, and he wants you to call him."

She replied, "I will."

"The doctor also said I was there for clearance for surgery. I'm confused."

And she said, "I am too! I will have to follow up with your adjuster and the physician on Monday."

As the pressure built up with me trying to find out what's going on with my body, I reached out on Thursday, June 6, 2019, to my employer nurse case manager with a text asking if there was any word to what was going on.

"Am I going to get the help? I need to correct my problems I'm dealing with or is it permanent damage?"

She replied, "We are waiting on the IME report. The physician you saw was asked to give his opinion regarding treatment options, etc. Once the report is received, we will be able to move forward on his recommendations. Usually, it takes about fourteen days after the appointment for us to receive it."

And I said, "Okay, I'm trying my best to stay out of the emergency room. These headaches that come and go, on and off every day be killing me. I changed my diet and everything, but nothing seems to work."

She said, "I'm sorry. I hate that you're having to deal with that. Do not hesitate, however, to seek treatment at an ER if needed. Hopefully we will get good direction as how to take care of you."

While waiting and anticipating this IME report, life still went on. Nothing stopped. Pains were still there. Medications weren't helping at all. Neglecting sleep at night, being tormented by the fears of death still. Headaches consuming my thoughts. Burning pains that throbbed and pulsated up and down my right arm and side, along with stabbing pains. This hand that I was dealt if it was spades, I would throw the whole hand away.

Thursday, June 13, 2019, I took a trip to downtown DC to the courthouse to my scheduled court date to modify my child support I was paying for my daughter. There was no way I can pay what I was paying before my accident. I didn't know what it was, but every time I get inside a court house and stand before a judge, I'm overwhelmed by anxiety and nervousness. I just knew that this attorney general that I was about to see was the same one that been at my throat ever since I had been fighting this custody battle for my son last year.

To my surprise, it wasn't him. It was a woman. While talking to the attorney general about modifying my child support, I showed her all my medical papers and explained what happened to me. She agreed and made adjustments, but the only problem was that my ex-wife did not show up. She did not know that she had to be there. The attorney general gave her a call and told her what was going on and if she agreed with the amount. And I said, "Can I pay it directly to you monthly?" And my ex-wife said yes.

And the attorney General and I walked in to the courtroom to see the judge. The last time I stood in front of the judge, I was fighting for custody of my son. That particular judge I felt that he had it out for me, but luckily, I didn't have him this go around. I had a lady judge, and the Attorney General told her what was going on and why, and the judge agreed with her and that it felt like a heavy load was lifted off my chest. I couldn't believe that my ex-wife agreed to lowering my support. I know it got to be due to my conditions and all I'm going through.

Monday, June 17, 2019, at 11:13 a.m. I texted my employer nurse case manager and said, "Good morning, any word yet?"

And she replied, "I have been on site this morning, and I don't see any results yet. I will keep checking."

At 12:35 p.m., she text me back and said, "It's in, and I forwarded a copy to your attorney. The IME doctor agrees with cervical spine surgery if cleared by the cardiologist."

Monday, June 24, 2019, my employer nurse case manager texted me saying that she would be emailing everyone with the same info but had me scheduled to see a third neurologist on the twenty-sixth at 1:30 p.m. in Virginia. I have not had any luck with neurologist. Here it was about to be the month of July, and I still didn't have any answers about what was going on with my body and what caused my injury. I was still not believing that I was allergic to lidocaine. I would not accept it. I just know deep down in my heart that the anesthesiologist and that doctor did something wrong rushing due to the fact of being late during the epidural procedure. I was just going to pray on it.

Wednesday, June 26, 2019, Yani took off from work, so she could go with me to see the new neurologist. When we arrived, I checked in, and we waited to be called. This time I had a pretty good feeling about this visit. No anxiety or nervousness while waiting. Finally an assistant called us to the back to be seated in a room, and the new neurologist came in and introduced herself to Yani and I. She did not waste any time. She got right to the point. She took my vitals and then asked what was going on with me and the reason for my visit. I did not hesitate and told her about my cardiac arrest during the epidural procedure and the balancing issues, the stuttering and forgetfulness, the confusion I was experiencing, and the excruciating headaches.

She then gave me a form for balancing and to get a MRI done and scheduled me for another appointment. During the drive home, Yani and I discussed the visit with the new neurologist. She definitely seemed like she knew what she was doing and seemed like she knew her stuff. I definitely think she was the one. Thank you, Jesus. I sent a text to my employer nurse case manager to let her know that the neurologist wanted me to go and get some physical therapy to help correct my balancing issue and also a cervical MRI done, and if she you could authorization from the worker's compensation adjuster.

My next appointment was scheduled for July 12 at 10:00 a.m. She replied, "I sure will reach out and get it taken care of. Did you like her?"

She asked, and I said, "Yes, I like her already."

She replied, "Good!"

"Thanks a million for finding this neurologist." She said that this neurologist was highly recommended, and she asked if she gave me any restrictions and if I was still off from work.

And I replied, "No, she just asked was I working right now."

And she said, "Okay and thank you."

Thursday, June 27, 2019, at 12:26 p.m., I reached out to my employer nurse case manager to let her know that I scheduled the MRI myself for July 8, 2019, and that I was just waiting on the authorization and I could start physical therapy the following day. She said thanks for letting her know. At 3:59 p.m., I texted her back to let her know that authorization was given for the MRI and they rescheduled it for the following day.

And she said, "Ooh, even better!" I told her that the cardiologist wanted me to get a sonogram, and I got an appointment scheduled for Monday, July 1, at hospital number one in Maryland. I was just waiting for authorization.

She replied, "Okay, thanks. I will bug your adjuster."

On the twenty-eight of June, I started physical therapy, which I felt that this should have been given to me right after my cardiac arrest. Also, I took care of getting the MRI. On Saturday, June 29, 2019, Yani wanted to do something nice for the kids, and I had my daughter for the weekend, so we went to Giant Foods and purchased some Six Flags tickets to take our two boys and our baby girl.

After arriving at the amusement park, the kids wanted to get on everything. They also wanted me to ride with them, but every ride had a sign stating that if you have any heart conditions to not attempt to ride. But I didn't let it bring me down. As long as our kids were enjoying themselves, smiling, laughing, and playing, I was content with their happiness as I shed a tear.

Sunday, June 30, 2019, Yani wanted me to go to the Honda dealership with her to purchase a new car, so I accompanied her. And the first thing I asked her was how much was she putting down, and she said, "Nothing. Watch me work."

And I said, "Yeah, okay." And sure enough, we drove out of the dealership in a brand new 2019 Honda Accord Sport. I couldn't believe it. When God's grace is upon you, the blessings will pour. She didn't put anything down and walked out that dealership an owner of a new 2019 Honda Accord Sport. On Monday, July 1, 2019, at 11:24 a.m., my employer nurse case manager texted me and asked if I had my scan that morning and when I would do a follow-up to get the results.

"P.S. Good morning."

And I responded, "Good morning, and the follow-up appointment is on the tenth of July."

And she said, "Okay, sounds excellent! I'm moving jobs, and my last day is Wednesday, so another nurse will be stepping in. I will get her contact info for you. I wish you the best, Kenny!"

At that moment, I did not know what to do. I mean, this lady actually cared about my well-being. I don't put my trust in a lot of people and especially strangers, but I did just that. Her and my new neurologist were the only ones I trusted then. I didn't even trust my cardiologist. After wiping a tear from my eye, I replied to the text, "Awww, thanks. I'm going to miss you. I've been taking this journey with you since day one. It's not going to be the same. I really appreciate all that you have done to help me."

She replied, "I know. I feel the same way. You are one of the strings that I'm leaving untied, and it kills me. I do feel like we have gotten you to a good place with the new neurologist, and you are so welcome."

This wasn't going to be good at all. Just when things seem like they were getting good and she stepped down. I know for a fact that I'm going to have problems. I just know it. Wednesday, July 3, 2019, at 12:43 p.m. I was finally getting a text message from the worker's compensation RN field case manager that went MIA on me when I went to Baltimore the first of June for insurance purposes only. Now she wants to communicate. Like really! She asked how my appointment was with the neurologist, and I said it was okay. And she sent me to physical therapy for balancing finally and had to hit her with the lol, then I said, "Yeah, I been asking for it for a while."

Yeah, this lady lost all my trust from here on out ever since I haven't heard from her since June 1. Oh yeah, we definitely had been playing a different game now. I said, "I see her again on the twelfth."

She replied, "Yup, I got all the doctor notes, MRI scans, and PT notes! Did you start PT yet?" And I told her yes, and she said, "Okay, great." But she was asking me if I started PT yet but got the notes saying that I started PT. Like, who does that?

Well, anyway, I got a text from my employer nurse case manager at 1:00 p.m., and she said, "Just wanted to reach out on my last day to tell you to take care! I will continue to send you healing energy and white light. God bless." And I told her thanks and I appreciate all she had done for me, and she said, "My pleasure," and gave me her personal number to keep in touch and to keep tabs on my healing.

Friday evening, July 5, 2019, Yani and I spent the evening looking up homes online down south to possibly relocate and change our surroundings to escape the traffic and clutter of the DMV. On Thursday evening, July 11, 2019, Yani and I spent time researching supplements, foods, and products that support liver regeneration and repair. I was not wasting any more time waiting on worker's compensation. Yani and I believed I might have suffered some type of ischemic injury to my liver during my cardiac arrest.

Green tea, grapefruit, grapes, cruciferous vegetables, nuts, and fatty fish are some foods to promote liver health. Milk thistle, turmeric root, dandelion root, beetroot, selenium, and ginger are some supplements that produce liver health also. We made a list of the foods to put on the grocery list so that we can pick up at Walmart after my appointment tomorrow.

Friday, July 12, 2019, I had an appointment with my neurologist, and right after my appointment, we took a trip down south to spend Yani's birthday weekend with her parents. Wednesday, July 17, 2019 at 10:21 a.m., the worker's compensation RN field case manager text me and asked me what the neurologist said at my appointment. I told her, "She asked me some questions concerning my pains and increased my meds on gabapentin and I go back in two weeks. And the cardiologist is looking at more of my blood work due to my liver still showing possible signs of damage. My liver enzymes are leaking into my bloodstream and are increasing, and I haven't been drinking any alcohol. My blood work taking during my cardiac arrest also shows a rapid increase of my white blood cells."

She replied, "Okay, I'm going to email your new insurance adjuster." And I told her "okay."

At 12:49 p.m., she texted me again asking me when I would see my neurologist again, and I told her on the twenty-sixth. She said, "Okay, I will see you there." Me already knowing her by now, I won't hold my breath. Wednesday, July 24, 2019, at 10:00 a.m. was my appointment with my cardiologist, and he was still baffled with my blood work and my liver enzymes. He kept asking me if I was drinking and doing illegal drugs. He really didn't believe that I stopped drinking in February of 2019.

At 5:22 p.m., I texted my worker's compensation RN field case manager to let her know that I had to reschedule my appointment and that the new appointment would be on August 9 at 9:45 a.m. My father-in-law passed away Friday of last week, and his going home service was scheduled for that Friday. She replied, "Okay, I'm sorry to hear that."

I wasn't expecting my father-in-law to pass. I was really looking forward to spending more time with him. He loved music just like I did. That was Yani and Jay's world. I know for a fact that this was going to be a devastating blow to them and my mother-in-law. Now I'm praying extra hard for God to give me the strength to fight through my pains and disabilities to be the rock for them to lean on if they need to. It hurt my heart to see Yani in so much pain. Any other time, I'm Yani's superman. I mean that I can fix just about anything, but one thing I can't fix is grief. All I could do was be a shoulder for her to cry on and to take care of Dad's baby girl.

I got her, Daddy. Your baby girl is in good hands. You already knew that when you stamped our union with your blessings. Rest in heavenly peace, Dad.

Thursday, July 25, 2019, I emailed my new employer nurse case manager number two and let her know that I talked to my cardiologist and he recommended that I see a liver specialists. My liver enzymes kept spiking and that wasn't normal. He suggested I go to hospital number eight in DC or go see anyone affiliated with that hospital. Also my primary care physician referred me to a specialist after I told him what my cardiologist said, and he wrote me a referral for one. And I asked her if she had any recommendations. And she said, "I copied your field case manager for further assistance." To me, it seemed like they didn't want me to see a liver specialist.

The morning of Dad's going home service was upon us, and the family wore his favorite color, which was royal blue. And when I say we looked sharp in that color, we looked sharp. The ladies and the guys made that royal blue radiate for Dad. Aunt Tia and Uncle

Jeff preached a good sermon. It hurt me to the heart to see my wife mourn for her daddy, and I couldn't fix the situation.

Monday, July 29, 2019, I emailed my new employer case nurse number two to let her know that I had to pay for my prescriptions at the pharmacy, and usually worker's compensation paid for it. She said, "I have forwarded to your adjuster. Thank you."

And in no time, my adjuster said, "The reimbursement will be in the mail tomorrow as follows." She also asked if I needed a new pharmacy card, and I said yes.

On August 1, 2019, I didn't know what was going on with my stomach, but I was having abdominal pains real bad. It got to the point that I couldn't deal with the pains anymore, and around 10:00 p.m., we checked in at the emergency room at hospital number 4. They took my vitals. My blood pressure was 108/56, and my weight was 165 pounds, temperature 98.3 F, pulse 53, respiration 15, and oxygen saturation 98 percent. They gave me some Toradol and took a sonogram of my stomach. Well, once again, they couldn't help me. They couldn't find a cause for my pains and discharged me.

While leaving, I looked at my lab results and my AST (SGOT) was 73 U/L, and it shouldn't be higher than 34 U/L, and my ALT was 182 U/L when it shouldn't be higher than 55 U/L. Now I know these have to do with my liver enzymes. Looking at this, I knew for a fact something is wrong. Also, my WBC, which is my white blood cells, was 9.73 U/L, and it should not be higher than 9.50 U/L. My ABS Lymph was 4.01 U/L and should not be higher than 3.22 U/L, and my ABS Mono was 0.93 U/L and should not be higher than 0.85 U/L.

I mean, I'm no doctor or nothing, but I saw something wrong. It was right on my paperwork. I mean, come on now! So of course, you know I was researching all of this when I got home. I was losing sleep due to trying to get to the bottom of this. *Is my liver damaged also?* This was the number one question that I need answered.

Friday, August 2, 2019, I emailed my new employer case nurse and let her know that I had to go to the emergency room due to abdominal pains and lower back pains. I let her know they did an ultrasound and everything looked normal but my liver enzymes and white blood cell count were still high, and they discharged me still in pain. She replied, "Sorry to hear that, Mr. Hough." I've copied field case nurse on this email. And as usual she was a no-show. No response or nothing.

Thursday, August 8, 2019 at 3:17 p.m., my worker's compensation RN field case manager text me and said, "Any paperwork you get from your appointment tomorrow, take a pic, and text it to me so your benefits can continue okay?"

I said, "Okay."

She replied, "I heard you were in the emergency room. I hope you're okay."

Now I'm a little frustrated and responded by saying, "YES, I'm in pain every day! My entire abdominal area and lower back, but they keep telling me everything is normal except my liver enzymes!"

She said, "I know, and I'm sorry."

I said, "No need to be. It isn't your fault. I appreciate it, though. Thanks."

And she said, "You will get through this. I know you will! I pray for you."

If that was only genuine, but I didn't believe her. She didn't care about my well-being. I know this for a fact. If she did, she would be coming to my appointments and not missing them.

Friday, August 9, 2019, I had my appointment with the neurologist, and she discussed my MRI results with me and wanted me to get another one with and without contrast. She saw an abnormal sign or artifact on my MRI. At 10:17 p.m., I texted the RN field case manager and let her know they gave me another prescription for 300 milligrams of gabapentin and wanted me to get another MRI. This time the upper back and they would email me an assessment of today's visit and that I would send it to her.

And she responded, "Perfect. I will update your adjuster." I told her that my next appointment would be August 23 at 10:00 a.m. Let us see if she would come.

Saturday, August 10, 2019, I had my baby girl for the weekend, which Baby Girl is actually her nickname. Yani figured we should get out the house and do something interactive with the kids, so we went out Virginia to go putt-putt golfing. We actually had a great time competing against each other.

Wednesday, August 14, 2019, at 1:38 p.m., my worker's compensation RN field case manager texted me and said, "Hey, let me know when your MRI will be, okay?" And I told her that I didn't know because my old employer case nurse took care of all that stuff for me. The new case nurse didn't do none of that, so how was I supposed to proceed? Was I supposed to schedule it? She said she talked to my new employer case manager, and she wanted me to do it. She also said, "Let me try to, okay?" I told her okay. If she wanted to do it then fine, but to be on the safe side, I better schedule one also.

Thursday, August 15, 2019, I texted her back at 9:12 a.m. and said, "Good morning. I got the MRI scheduled for Thursday, August 22, at 10:45 a.m. They going to contact my adjuster for authorization."

At 10:40 a.m., she responded, "Okay, great!" At 12:49 p.m., I texted her again to let her know that they changed the date to August 27 at 2:15 p.m. She asked, "Did you have a cardiologist appointment yesterday?" I said yes, and she said, "What did he say? Any paperwork? Text it to me so I can update your adjuster." I told her that he took my blood work and would do another ultrasound of my heart on my next appointment to see if it's any improvement and he didn't give me any paperwork but that I could get it for her on my next appointment.

She asked, "When is your next appointment?" I told her on October 4 at 10:00 a.m. She said, "Okay, perfect. What's his name? Sorry." Really though? How do you forget my cardiologist's name, and I had been seeing him since April? So I give her his name, and she said, "That's right."

I said, "I had to google it for the spelling."

And said, "Me too!"

I asked, "Since my neurologist appointment is before my MRI appointment, should I reschedule my neurologist appointment?"

And she said, "Yeah, that might be a good idea."

I said, "Okay. I will let you know the new date."

Tuesday, August 20, 2019 at 2:32 p.m., I texted the worker's compensation RN field case nurse to let her know that my neurologist appointment was scheduled for August 28 at 10:30 a.m., the day after MRI appointment. And she said, "Okay."

Tuesday, August 27, 2019, I went to the radiology center in Maryland to get my MRI and to kill all speculations that I had about what this scan was going to reveal to me. I was still not believing that I was allergic to lidocaine and that caused my cardiac arrest. I was thinking that either the epidural needle broke off into my spinal cord or they went too deep with the needle. While lying inside the scanning machine, the back of my neck got extremely hot, and this was the first time I actually experienced this after all the times I have been in this machine due to my injury. I couldn't wait to get out of the machine so I can start researching my experience I just had.

I told Yani what had happened, and she just said, "Let's just wait for the results, baby." For some odd reason, I was really believing that this could be the cause of my cardiac arrest. Either it's a piece of needle in my spine or they went too far with the needle puncturing my spinal cord or the anesthesiologist gave me too much medicine in my IV.

Thursday, August 29, 2019 at 12:39 p.m., my worker's compensation RN field case manager texted me and said, "How did your appointment go yesterday?" And I told her that my neurologist haven't gotten back the MRI results from the radiologist yet and that she would call me once she got them. Other than that, she increased my dosage of gabapentin and took me off the other medication and gave me a new one. I told her I would let her know when they contact me. She asked if I had any other appointments for the neurologist in the future. And I responded yes on September 9 at 10:30 a.m. to do a nerve study and follow-up appointment right after. She said, "Perfect."

And I said, "Oh, also, while I was getting the MRI, my upper back got extremely hot!"

She said, "Did you tell them that?"

I said, "I told my neurologist."

She said, "Okay, good. Not sure if contrast was used. That's normal." I told her that contrast was used, but all other times getting MRI I never felt that. She said, "Oh okay!"

Friday, August 30 2019, I got my MRI results in the mail and emailed an attachment of it to my new employer case nurse so she could forward it to my worker's compensation crew, my RN field case manager, and adjuster. After reading over the results, I had a few questions pertaining to the results myself. I needed to find out what CSF intensity lesion is and what is syringomyelia. These were on my results so you know I had to go to Google to find out until my next neurologist appointment. So upon my research, I deemed that the CSF intensity lesion happened due to the placement of the epidural needle. CSF is cerebral spinal fluid, and an epidural can cause damage to the spinal cord.

Syringomyelia is fluid-filled cyst within your spinal cord. And in my case, it developed from trauma. I was also curious about what a nerve study was and how they can detect damaged nerves. I couldn't wait until my appointment to see how this would be done.

Friday, September 6, 2019, Yani took me to get this nerve study done. After checking in, the assistant had me come back to a room and had me lay on some type of medical bed and remove my shirt, and the nurse took measurements based on my height and fastened some metal disc electrodes to certain areas of my arm and a shock-emitting electrode also. Then she stuck some type of needle into my muscles in my arm, and it sent electrical pulses to my nerves. And she wrote down and recorded the results to show the doctor.

I guess something wasn't right, and the nurse said she would be right back and went to get the doctor. They both came into the room, and the doctor wanted to see for himself the readings, and he started sticking me with the needle to see the results. He then said that yes, I did have pinched nerves in my arm and wrote my assessment stating the EMG of selected right C5 to T1 innervated muscles showed large units with decreased recruitment in triceps and it was abnormal findings and that there was electro diagnostic evidence for chronic right radiculopathy. After doing the nerve study, I was taken to another room to talk to my neurologist, and she asked me a few questions about my pains and increased my medication of gabapentin. Also, I was recommended for physical therapy for twenty-one days, and once again, my worker's compensation RN field case nurse was a no-show.

At 12:05 p.m., she texted me and said, "Hey, I tried to make it today to your appointment, but I had to cover for my boss this morning. How did your appointment go today?" I told her that my appointment was to get the nerve study done. My follow-up appointment would on the thirteenth of September at 9:30 p.m. I really didn't believe her. At this point, I didn't even care if she came to my appointments or not. Yani was fed up with my worker's compensation field case manager, and since they never granted authorization for me to see a liver specialist after I kept asking, Yani scheduled me an appointment at 1:00 p.m. on September 10, 2019, at hospital number eight.

I didn't have to wait any longer. Yani went ahead and used our personal insurance provider since worker's compensation wasn't trying to give authorization. They took my vitals, which my blood pressure was 99/59, weight 167 pounds, temperature 98.1, pulse 77, respiration 18, and oxygen saturation was 96 percent. I talked with the doctor and explained my situation that resulted in my cardiac arrest. She took out her stethoscope and took a listen to my chest, stomach, and back, and ordered a seventeen-item blood test to check my liver for everything, including Hepatitis A, B, and C. They took my blood right there, and the doctor said she would notify me if she saw something that wasn't right or if I needed a liver biopsy, she would contact me.

On Monday, September 23, 2019, at 3:10 p.m., my worker's compensation RN field case manager texted me and said, "Hey, how did your neurologist appointment go today?" I told her that I did not have an appointment that day and that I won't see my neurologist until October 11. She said, "I am screwing up left and right."

Friday, October 4, 2019, at 11:00 a.m., I went to see my cardiologist, and he talked with me a bit about my diet and still didn't believe that I was not drinking and doing drugs. He did an ultrasound of my heart and liver, took some blood samples, and sent me on my way. At 2:25 p.m., my worker's compensation RN field case manager texted me and said, "Did you have a visit with the cardiologist today? If so, how did it go?" I told her that my appointment went okay and my cardiologist said that my heart showed a big improvement and my lower wall was still slightly damaged but should be fully healed in about a year. He also took some blood for testing to see if my liver enzymes came down. She replied, "Okay, great."

Saturday morning, October 5, 2019, Yani took me to the pharmacy to pick up my prescriptions, but they were still using my personal insurance instead of charging worker's compensation. It's definitely an inconvenience to stand in line all this time and you couldn't get your meds. So I emailed my new employer case nurse and said, "I don't know what this pharmacy is doing, but I'm showing them the insurance card provided by worker's compensation, and they still charging the prescriptions to my personal insurance. I tell them I will be back in a couple of days, and when I come back, they still don't have the situation fixed!"

She replied, "Hey, Mr. Hough. I've copied your new nurse case manager on this email. You can contact her moving forward." All I could say was wow! I wondered what else was going to change.

Monday morning, October 7, 2019, the new case nurse number three responded to my email. "Good morning. Thank you for the email. I'm sorry you are having difficulties at the pharmacy. I have forwarded your message on to the claims adjuster and your field case manager so that we can work together on resolving this for you. Have a good day!" I was thinking to myself after seeing her email maybe things would go much smoother while she was at the helm now. I mean I was on employer case nurse number three now!

At 1:45 p.m., I had an appointment with my neurologist. She took my vitals, blood pressure 108/70, pulse 75, and weight was 162 pounds. I was having pains in my left arm and persistent severe pain in the right arm. Left arm pain was from the neck down, and the right arm pain was burning. I was taking 5400 milligrams of gabapentin a day, but it wasn't effective. I was having difficulties sleeping at night. I was experiencing severe headaches all day. I could not turn my neck certain ways. And I was still walking with a cane. My neurologist started me taking 200 milligrams of Lyrica three times a day and 60 milligrams of Cymbalta twice a day.

Friday, October 11, 2019, the new employer case nurse number three emailed me and said that my new worker's compensation adjuster emailed her an update that they would call the pharmacy to review the process of processing medications through worker's compensation. This should resolve the problem. If I have continued issues to have the pharmacy call them. And that my new adjuster mentioned to her that he mailed me a replacement pharmacy card just to make sure it has the correct information.

Saturday, October 12, 2019, I got a medical bill in the mail, so I scanned it and emailed it to Julia and asked if she could forward it to my new adjuster. She said, "Absolutely, I'll forward it to your adjuster. Have a good day."

At 2:11 p.m. on Wednesday, October 16, 2019, the RN field case manager texted me and asked what the neurologist said. I was to the point now that I didn't even feel like talking to her anymore! I just wished she did her job and either come to my appointments or contact my doctors directly. I went and told her anyway. I said, "My neurologist said I have two options, either pain management or surgery."

She said, "Okay, but the cardiologist have not cleared you for surgery, correct?"

I said, "Oh, I don't know. My next appointment with the cardiologist is December 6."

She said, "Okay. Sorry, I'm driving. When is your next neurologist appointment?" I told her it was November 11.

On Friday, October 18, 2019, I got an email from my third employer case nurse, and she said, "Good morning, Kenny. I received an email from your new adjuster responding to the final request for payment that you forward it to us." He said, "I just called the provider and provided the worker's compensation information. They have updated the bill and records. Thanks and have a nice weekend."

Thursday, October 24, 2020, I sent an email to my employer case nurse to say that I was still having problems at the pharmacy with my medications. The pharmacy was charging my personal insurance and trying to get me to pay the balance out of pocket. The pharmacy was calling worker's compensation for authorization, and the medications weren't being authorized. I told her I was running out of my heart medications, carvedilol, 12.5 milligrams, and valsartan, 80 milligrams. I had enough until the next day, and then I would be out. She responded back and said thanks for letting her know, and she forwarded my email to the adjuster. And in no time, she emailed me back and said the adjuster explained that the issue had been corrected.

The weekend of Halloween, my wife and mother-in-law had planned a trip to Universal Studios in Florida for our son's sixteenth birthday, and we had to fly, so I had to get clearance from my cardiologist first. I gave him a call, and he said it was okay. I really need this getaway.

On Monday, November 11, 2019, the worker's compensation RN field case manager texted me at 1:33 p.m. and said, "How did it go today?" At this point, I'm not even in the mood today for her bull crap, so I didn't even respond to her text. Thursday, November 14, 2019, I emailed my employer case nurse the assessment report from my neurologist and asked if she could forward it to my adjuster and the RN field case manager. I also attached a referral to see a neurosurgeon for a second opinion of my options resulting in my injury and that I need authorization, please and thank you.

And in no time, she responded and said, "Good morning," and she forward the email to the corresponding parties and asked if the referral was authorized. I was glad I could depend on her. She stayed on point. I haven't had a problem with her yet. I let a whole week go by, and I called the neurosurgeon's office and asked if worker's compensation authorized me to be seen for an appointment, and they said no. So I scheduled an appointment myself for December 12, and if worker's compensation wouldn't authorize my appointment, I would use my own insurance at this point. I still haven't got closure on what happened on February 15, 2019 that caused my cardiac arrest and nerve damage, and I ain't buying that I'm allergic to lidocaine crap. I emailed my employer case nurse and let her know the situation and that I still need authorization. And she said that she forwarded the message to my adjuster and the worker's compensation RN field case manager.

Monday, December 2, 2019 at 3:53 p.m., the RN field case manager texted me and said, "Hey. So I requested your adjuster to send authorization to the neurosurgeon's office so you can be seen on December 11 and will follow up with him in the morning as well."

I said, "Okay. Thanks."

She said, "And your cardiologist appointment is tomorrow, right? I'm going to try to make it because I have an early office visit in Baltimore."

I told her that my cardiologist appointment would be December 6 and that I already scheduled my appointment with the neurosurgeon on December 10 at 3:30 p.m. And she didn't respond back until 8:54 p.m. "Okay. Perfect."

Friday, December 6, 2019 at 2:44 p.m., my worker's compensation RN field case manager texted me and said, "Hey, how did your cardiologist appointment go? Did he give you any paperwork? If so, take a picture and text it to me." I told her that my appointment went okay and no, there was no paperwork. Thinking to myself, *Since she ain't doing her job, why should I ask for paperwork anyway? I ain't planning on getting any surgery! That option is dead! They won't kill me twice!*

She said, "Okay, you're still not cleared heart-wise, and did he do any blood work?" I told her yes, and she said, "Okay, thanks. I'm off today because my son is finally having his heart surgery in the morning." Now I didn't know this, and I have a heart filled with passion and sympathy when it comes to situations like this and especially for kids.

So I said, "Oh wow. Sorry to hear that. My prayers are with you and your family."

She said, "Thank you. He was born prematurely and had a heart murmur, but last week, he ended up getting pneumonia, so we had to wait until it cleared up to be cleared for surgery. When do you see the cardiologist again?" I told her on the twenty-sixth to pick up a portable heart monitor to wear for a week and follow-up appointment January 6, 2020. She said, "Ok, I'll call his office to get anything I need to send to the adjuster. Thanks, Ken."

Tuesday, December 10, 2019, Yani took me out to Virginia to see the neurosurgeon. We arrived at his office and signed in and gave the receptionist my MRI discs. At 3:05 p.m., I got a text from the worker's compensation RN field case manager, and she said, "Hey, I'm on I-95 hoping to get there. But if I don't make it, just go and see him." I was thinking to myself, *Am I not supposed to see the doctor because she is not here?* I already know she ain't coming.

Finally, I was called back to see the neurosurgeon, and Yani accompanied me to a room on the right. And we sat down, and the doctor introduced himself and got straight to the point. He said that I had two options: either I can live with the injury forever and hope it won't get any serious than it already was or get cervical discectomy fusion surgery, which has a 90 percent success rate, but it wouldn't guarantee that it would correct my issue.

Well, this was all that I needed to hear. Now I just had to wait until I saw my neurologist so I could get the necessary documents that my attorney needs to get this ball rolling. At 9:05 p.m. the worker's compensation RN field case manager texted me and said, "Hey, sorry I tried to get there today. What did the neurosurgeon say?"

"He said that I have two options," and I told her what those two options were.

And she said, "Okay. Yeah, the cervical dissection has a good success rate. I just wonder if you can get this done with your cardiologist. I wonder if you can be cleared to get this done. What are your feelings on it? Yeah, I got there after you had just left, they said." I just looked at the message and became irritated.

Saturday, December 28, 2019, I went to my pharmacy to pick up my prescriptions, and once again, I was having the same issues with authorizations. I know it was not the pharmacy's fault. Besides, the staff had always been sweet to me. So I sent an email to my employer case nurse because I knew she could rectify the issue in a timely manner. In my email I said, "Hey, I hate to bother you, but why is it every time I fill my prescriptions, worker's compensation isn't giving authorizations and making my life more miserable and complicated than what it is already? It's not my fault that this accident happened to me. I've been dealing with this inconvenience ever since March of 2019. It's tiresome and draining. The main medication I need is my heart medications, and I'm not getting authorization, and I run out tonight! This is crazy! I'm sick and tired of it!"

Monday, December 30, 2019 at 2:35 p.m., I got a text from my worker's compensation RN field case manager, and she said, "I just saw an email about your meds. I just escalated it to someone to help you with this. I'm sorry."

I was at the end of my rope with this lady and the worker's compensation adjuster due to getting authorizations. I didn't even respond to her text.

Thursday, January 2, 2020. It had been five whole days and still no refill authorization for Valsartan, 80 milligrams, my heart medication, so I shot my employer case nurse an email saying I really need my medications. On Monday, January 6, 2020, I got an email from my employer case nurse, and she said, "Hey, I got an email update from your adjuster. This should be resolved moving forward. He also said if there are any issues while at the pharmacy, have them call." Now this sounded like music to my ears, and I thanked her for her help.

Tuesday, January 7, 2020, I got a text from the RN field case manager, and she said, "Hey, Ken. Hope you're doing well. How did your visit go for the heart monitor? Did they ever fix your medication issue? Are you able to talk? I was off your case, and now I'm back on it. I'm working from home. If you need anything, please don't hesitate."

And once again, I didn't respond. I was thinking to myself, *If she was off my case, she should have stayed off it.* Why haven't they replaced her like they did everyone else. Tuesday, January 28, 2020, the RN field case manager texted me at 4:19 p.m. and said, "I just wanted to check in with you. How are you doing?" And once again, no response from me.

Friday, January 31, it was finally here. All that was going on with my body from the cardiac arrest, and I made it to see my forty-third birthday. Usually, I would be in party mode, but since I quit drinking and all the headaches and nerve pains I was dealing with just killed my spirit. I didn't want to do anything at all but lay in the bed and take my medications for my pains. My wife didn't see it that way and wanted us to celebrate my birthday. She demanded me to get up and get dressed. She got me the Jordan Retro 11 with the metallic color change and a matching shirt and took me to my favorite spot, Longhorn Steak House. With the birthday love that my wife gave me, it put me back in good spirits, and I really enjoyed our outing. I got my usual, The Porterhouse with a fully loaded baked potato and a house salad. Yani got a New York Strip with the same sides also.

Sunday, February 2, 2020, usually Yani would ask me if I would go to church with her. But on this particular day, I just felt a need to show gratitude to my maker for letting me see another birthday despite being a statistic of dying after recovering from my cardiac arrest. I voluntarily told Yani that I would be attending service with her, and we went to church and attended the noon service. The choir started singing a few song selections to begin service. After a few songs and praise, the Holy Spirit was strong in the atmosphere that you could feel the anointing in the air. I mean, you could feel the presence of the Lord real heavy up in that place. I never felt anything like it in my life. It felt like this service was meant for me. I mean that this service was talking to my soul. The choir sang a song saying that you could do anything but fail when it comes to Jesus.

Then Reverend Wilson came up and spoke on whatever you're going through, all things are possible through Jesus. She also gave us a word from Ephesians 6:10–14 that said:

> My brethren, be strong in the Lord and in the power of his might, put on your whole armor of God, that you may be able to stand against the wiles of the devil, for we do not wrestle against flesh and blood, but against principalities, against powers, against the rulers of the darkness of this age, against spiritual hosts of wickedness in the heavenly places. Therefore take up

the whole armor of God that you may be able
to withstand in the evil day, and having to done
all to stand. Stand therefore, having girded your
waist with truth, having put on the breastplate of
righteousness.

Deacon King then came up and said a short prayer, giving
thanks to the Lord for allowing us to wake up and anoint the minis-
try and pastor, and he said, "The Lord loves us all collectively." Then
the church asked all the new visitors to stand, and we all greeted
them with warm welcomes. The message for today's service was
spiritual warfare. The choir sang another selection and then did the
announcements for the week and did tithes and offerings. The choir
then sang another selection about Jesus knows how much we can
bare.

When you're saved, "Can you remember the day that Jesus saved
you? Meeting Jesus is a life changing event," said Reverend Wilson.

Anthony lead the choir into another song selection, "I thought
I knew peace until I met Jesus. I thought I knew joy, and then I met
him. I thought I knew love until I met Jesus. I got a whole new life
when I met him. I was the one, someone told me to come, and Jesus
changed me. So if you are the one, just come and let Jesus change
you. Today is your day for a life change. Just try Jesus, you will never
be the same."

These words that Anthony and the choir were singing was really
talking to me. These words in this song were powerful. I could feel
God's love all on me. My eyes were even watery. Reverend Wilson
came back up and gave a short testimony relating to that powerful
song. She said how much her life changed after giving her life to
Christ. Don't take it for granted! She even cried while saying that.
Now it's time for the pastor as he came up, and he must have felt that
song deep like the way I felt the song so he asked the choir to sing
that song again. The spirit was moving so strongly up in there that
the pastor didn't even give us the word yet. He went straight to altar
call. Usually altar call is right after the word, but I guess God had
other plans on this day.

The Holy Spirit was really working that day as a child made his way by himself down to the altar. Such a young child at that with such bravery to maneuver his way through thousands of people to get right with God. The pastor stopped him and asked him his age, and he was just ten years old, and he also asked him why he came down to the altar. And the little boy said, "I want to give my life to Christ."

Wow as I thought to myself as the little boy's eyes were filled with tears. The pastor extended the invitation to the ones that know God but has backslid to come down and get right with God again. The pastor said, "I'm putting service on pause because God wants you to have insurance in him." He also said, "While the blood is still running warm in your veins to not fight it. Don't doubt it. Don't deny it. Just receive it."

The choir just kept singing but just stayed focus singing a phrase over and over again that went like this: "Today is your day for a life change. Just try Jesus, you'll never be the same."

I couldn't deny it any longer. I felt a love that I never felt before. Something was really moving me at this point. The pastor also extended the invitation to anyone who needed a church home. The pastor told everyone to come down to the altar that the angels were throwing down in glory and that this was the best thing that could ever happen in our lives that Jesus was going to take residency in us. God also loves backsliders and the ones that were looking for insurance from God will get it. The part that got me the most was that the pastor was talking about how some folk say that you don't have to belong to a church and that they are wrong. He said, "Don't make me go to the Bible and pull up the scripture on them. God wants everyone under the umbrella of a church," and extended the invitation for everyone that didn't belong to a church. That really touched me. I was the main one always saying that I didn't have to belong to church to get closer to God. Now I can't deny that God was talking to me on this day.

I felt something that I couldn't describe. I felt it all through my body. I tried to fight it, but the more I tried, the stronger it got. And eventually, it got the best of me, and I sprang to my feet. I moved away from my seat, passed Yani, and headed down the aisle toward the altar while walking with a limp due to my balancing was off from my injury. It caught the pastor's eye, and he asked me why I was limping. And I explained to him that last year while getting an epidural injection, something went wrong, and I went into cardiac arrest. The pastor stopped the music and spoke to the congregation and told them my testimony.

He said, "This is Kenny, and he is forty-three. And he was on the operating table, and he died for eight minutes. But he doesn't look dead to me. Isn't God good?" People were clapping and shouting, and I turned around, and Yani was standing right beside me with tears falling from her eyes as she gave me a big hug. And at that moment, it seemed the floodgates have opened up wide, and more people came down to the altar to give their life to Christ also.

I can't believe it's been almost an entire year since my cardiac arrest, and I wasn't a statistic. I pretty much been a ghost on social media, but on my one year anniversary on Saturday, February 15, 2020 at 9:15 a.m., I took to Facebook and said, "A year ago on this day changed my entire life. I was getting an epidural shot in my neck for a work-related injury and went into cardiac arrest. It's been a battle trying to get proper help for my complications while fighting with worker's compensation for authorizations. One particular worker's compensation nurse called me a statistic and counted me out.

"Many visits to the ER just to be told they can't help me. All the medications these doctors had me taking got me feeling like a zombie. The chest pains and headaches every day are driving me crazy. Permanent nerve damage is keeping me up all night with tears of pain running down my face and not getting any sleep. I was dealing with anxiety, depression, and mood swings because I can't do some of the things that I used to do. Having to concentrate just to walk and while I'm having a conversation just to speak. And all the doctor appointments to see my cardiologist and neurologist just for follow-ups.

"If I knew that this would have been my outcome, I would have not went through with the procedure. My wife was against me going, and she refused to take me on that dreadful day. And I called my little sister, Kesha, to take me and went anyway. Just to get there and wait for a late doctor. I saw all the signs and ignored them. I'm very thankful for my wife for being my support team through all of this pain and agony that I have been dealt. And also my mother-in-law, Tawana, and father-in-law, Steve. I love y'all. And also I want to thank family and friends that's been there for me and keeping me in their prayers."

Tuesday, February 25, 2020, I was still having authorization issues at the pharmacy, so I reached out to my employer case nurse and said, "Good morning, is it possible if you can let my claim adjuster know that I'm still having a hard time at the pharmacy to fill my prescription of amitriptyline 25 milligrams. My neurologist prescribed this medication for me."

She responded back and said, "Hi, Kenny! Thanks for letting me know. I forwarded this to your adjuster."

And I said, "Thanks, I really appreciate it."

Monday, March 9, 2020, I had a neurologist appointment, and during the assessment, I was asked about my headaches and if they had died down. And no, they were still kicking my butt day and night. I was told about a new drug on the market called Emgality and asked if I would consider taking it monthly to help suppress my headaches. And you know me, you don't have to ask me twice. I agreed, and the first dose, you have to take two shots in the stomach. The doctor injected the first shot, and Yani injected the second shot.

Around about this time, we, the DMV, which is known as the District of Columbia, Maryland, and Virginia area, that's close to one another were hit with the pandemic of the deadly COVID-19 virus. Places started closing down, and strict measures were starting to take place for essential businesses.

Wednesday, March 11, 2020, I emailed my employer case nurse and said, "Good morning. Is it possible to let my adjuster know that my neurologists prescribed me a new medication for my headaches? It's called Emgality, and it's injected into the stomach or thigh once a month, and the pharmacy needs authorization for this medication."

She said, "Good morning, Kenny. Absolutely, I'll forward this right now. Thank you."

I replied, "Great, thank you so much."

Friday, March 13, 2020, I was having more issues at the pharmacy with my medications again. You would have at least thought this would have been corrected by now. I reached out to my employer case nurse to let her know what was going on and I had five medications here to pick up, and they were carvedilol, 12.5 milligrams, and valsartan, 80 milligrams, which are my heart medications, and pregablin, 200 milligrams, amitriptyline, 25 milligrams, and duloxetine, 60 milligrams. These are my nerve medications.

The pharmacists were trying to call someone, but I don't think they were getting anywhere.

"Can you help me with this, please?"

She replied, "Good morning. The pharmacy can call worker's compensation if there are any further issues and can you provide me with a phone number for the pharmacy your adjuster can give them a call."

And I said, "Thank you."

Since I was quote, unquote supposed to be allergic to lidocaine, I postponed my dental checkups due to my situation, and during this time, a filling came out of my left bottom back molar, and it had been causing me some problems. Well, I couldn't take the pain no more, so on Tuesday, March 24, 2020, Yani scheduled me an appointment to get an emergency tooth extraction done.

Before the dentist did anything, I explained to him I was supposed to be allergic to lidocaine due to an epidural injection going wrong, and after hearing my story, the dentist decided that I wasn't allergic to lidocaine and pumped my gums full of it to extract my tooth. He had to at least give me over ten shots of lidocaine. I was afraid, but after he kept using the lidocaine, I knew I wasn't allergic. Well, guess that answers that question.

Thursday, May 7, 2020, I just woke up at 7:10 a.m. to use the bathroom, and as I sat up, all of a sudden, my brain felt as if it was spinning inside my skull. My head felt as if I was going to crash it into the floor. I grabbed on to the bed because I was unaware where I was due to the spinning. Yani asked me what was wrong, and I explained what happened. And we were both lost on what had transpired. This issue started to be an everyday occurrence, and on top of that, it would occur several times a day and make me feel nauseated.

Every time I sit up from lying down, I would get dizzy, and everything felt as if it was spinning real fast, and I would have to hold on to something to keep from falling. Even when I stood up from sitting down, I experienced the same event. The world felt like it was spinning too fast. I was dealing with this issue for weeks, and I got tired of it and wanted to get to the bottom of what it was that was causing me this issue. I grabbed my phone and went to my trusty favorite site, which is Google, and put in my symptoms, and my results pointed to vertigo.

Why, so now I got this on top of everything else I'm dealing with? Just great! What caused this? Now I got more anxiety and stress to deal with. Yani found some videos on YouTube to help me do some exercises to help me get rid of this vertigo. After continuous attempts, the exercises failed.

Monday, May 18, 2020, today was my son's, Kay's, eighteenth birthday and also my first appointment to see a pain specialist doctor. Yani took me to my appointment, and after telling the doctor my situation and what caused my condition, he prescribed me a medication called nabumetone, 500 milligrams, and physical therapy. Since we are in the middle of a pandemic, I was not trying to put myself in danger or my family in danger of being exposed to COVID-19 by continuing physical therapy, so that was a no go for me.

After dealing with this vertigo for some weeks now, I couldn't take it anymore. On Sunday, May 24, 2020, I emailed my neurologist saying that I hated to bother her on a Sunday and I knew we had an appointment coming up in June, but I had this problem I was dealing with that was bothering me, and I thought it would resolve itself on its own, but it hadn't. I first noticed it the beginning of this month, but it might have been longer. But I probably didn't recognize it. Lately if I was lying down in bed and I got up, I got real dizzy and light headed and had to stop and hold on to something because I felt like I was falling. If I sitting up and stand, I have the same experience. Even if I'm in the bed and turn onto my side, it felt like I was falling to the floor, and I had to close my eyes and hold on to the bed until it stopped, and I got real nauseated. Now that I was aware of it, this is a very frequent occurrence.

"Is this normal? And what is it? Also my headaches seemed to pick up more frequently now during this."

My neurologist didn't waste time and responded right back with an email and said, "Mr. Hough, are you able to check your blood pressure? If you can, please check it several times, especially around the times when I feel dizzy. We can move your appointment to Tuesday. Would you be able to do telemedicine appointment at 9:30 a.m.?"

I responded back and told her I could check my blood pressure and I could do a telemedicine or an office visit, whatever she has available, and at the present time, my blood pressure was 120/78, which was good because it's usually lower. During the course of the day, I had four more spells, and at 7:22 p.m. after the fourth spell, my blood pressure was 79/65 and pulse was 69.

Dealing with this, I was scared to move or get out of the bed. I was thinking to myself, *Man, I can't deal with this mess here*, as a tear rolled out of my eye. And I asked the Lord, *Why me, God? Why me?* Before the night was over, I had four other spells before I was able to go to sleep.

The next morning, my neurologist emailed me to let me know which office location she was at and I could come in at 9:30 a.m. if I could. She told me to also call my cardiologist to see if my heart medications might need to be decreased. But of course, I didn't get her email until 2:00 p.m. I was up all night because I couldn't sleep. I emailed her back that I couldn't sleep and stayed up all night due to the spinning and nausea and also apologized for missing the appointment and if it was possible for me to do a telemedicine appointment later. She responded and told me that we could do the appointment at 3:30 p.m. Came to find out, it was vertigo, and my neurologist increased my daily dosage of amitriptyline to rid me of the vertigo, and in a couple of days, it was gone.

Thursday, June 4 2020, I woke up early in the morning and started my usual activities. Friday, July 14, 2020, my wife, my son, and myself packed the car up with our belongings and headed to my

IME appointment with the insurance company doctor regarding my case. We took the fifty-minute drive headed to Reston, Virginia, to be there for my scheduled time of 8:45 a.m. I was nervous at first when I got there and was thinking that this doctor was going to be like the other doctor I had to see out Baltimore, Maryland, for the assessment that I had to do.

I was dealing with so much anxiety anticipating this meeting with this doctor that I haven't even planned anything for my wife's birthday, which was today also. Shame on me as I was thinking while sitting in the waiting room in the doctor's office. I was finally called back by the doctor, and I gave him my MRI discs. And as he was reviewing them, he made it perfectly clear that he was hired by the insurance company. He asked me some questions about my injury, and I told him, but it was a few things that I was dealing with that I forgot to tell him. At the end of the assessment, he wished me luck with my case. I didn't know how to take that. Did he mean that he was siding with the insurance company? Or was he siding with me?

I walked back to the car and told my son and wife what went down, and we headed out to go down south so my wife could spend her birthday with her mom and our son that's been staying with her for the summer and our niece, Nay Nay. This year was definitely challenging trying to celebrate birthdays during the pandemic since everything was pretty much shut down due to the pandemic.

Also, I wanted to give an update of my heart condition. When I had the cardiac arrest, the left ventricle of my heart was badly damaged, and the ejection fraction was the volumetric fraction of fluid ejected from the chamber with each contraction and the normal percentage was anything greater than fifty-five, and mine was below that, but I have another testimony to give now. I no longer take carvedilol or valsartan heart medications for my heart because my heart is 100 percent healed. Isn't God good? I'm a walking miracle.

I had fear of what happened to me and all I have been going through with my experience, but now the fear is gone, and I have been sharing my testimony with family and friends and even strangers. My spiritual eye is now open, and I have a better understanding of things that I once have not understood, especially a better understanding of when I was getting that epidural injection and I was in darkness with the unseen force, and it felt as though hands was all over my body trying to pull me down and hold me down. I was in a battle for my soul and life in spiritual warfare with the enemy, and God gave me a second chance to get it right.

About the Author

Kenneth Hough, author of *A 2nd Chance at Life*, was born in 1977, and raised in North Brentwood, Maryland, just eleven minutes from the District of Columbia. Fascinated with taking things apart and putting things together when he was younger, he had a career job installing elevators for eighteen years of his life.

Known as Kenny Keys by his peers, in his spare time when he wasn't working as an elevator mechanic, he was a local producer on the underground music scene and also a musician that played keyboards for bands in the DMV area, which is known as the District of Columbia, Maryland, and Northern Virginia.

Due to a work-related injury, he had a cardiac arrest while getting an epidural injection in his neck that changed his life forever.